BIG JOHN'S SPEEDWAY GRILL

Meredith® Books
Des Moines, Iowa

Book Design: After Hours Creative
Contributing Writers: Russ Haan, Eric Koski, Walt Smith
Principal Food Photography: Bill Harrison
Additional Food Photography: Tim Lanterman
Racing Images: David Chobat, Nigel Kinrade, Dorsey Patrick, Sam Sharpe
Additional Photography: Eric Koski, Tim Lanterman
Recipe Testing and Food Styling: Carol Konyha, Mike Oleskow

Meredith Books
1716 Locust Street
Des Moines, Iowa 50309–3023
www.meredithbooks.com

First Edition. Printed in the United States of America.
Library of Congress Control Number: 2005929462
ISBN: 0-696-22687-1

Dedication

I would like to dedicate this book to my parents, who went through hell and high water for us as children. Thanks to them, my two sisters and I never had to wish for anything. Somehow, my parents always managed to provide the necessities.

My parents and grandparents, who have all now passed on, grew up through the Great Depression. My parents experienced what it was like to hop a freight train to go pick huckleberries up the mountain. When they got home, my grandparents would confiscate most of the berries and sell them for a little bit of extra cash. But they always kept enough to make one pie.

I especially thank my mother and grandmother for letting me stay in the kitchen while they cooked. I thank my mother's father for teaching me how to build a junk empire. I am honored by how my father helped this great nation of ours stay free during WWII. He flew 31 missions in a B-17 over occupied France and Germany. He also risked his life before the war when he worked the coal mines in Luzerne County, Pennsylvania.

I am thankful to my father's parents, who fled Russia and came to Pennsylvania with only the clothes on their backs (and some recipes that were truly delicious, but I've never been able to duplicate)! I can only silently say thank you to them.

To my parents and grandparents—I wish you could see the finished cookbook!

Big John

How This Whole Thing Happened

Not too long ago my buddy Eric Koski and I were out hunting and talking smack about our jobs and lives. Since pretty much a chunk of my life has been spent at the NASCAR tracks, cooking for the teams and drivers, Eric asked me if I had ever thought of writing a cookbook. I had to laugh—I'm a big, crusty Polish redneck, and frankly, I wasn't sure I had much to offer in the way of cooking tips. Heck, I never even went to cooking school myself.

But you know what? The odds are you haven't been to cooking school either. Most of what I know about cooking I learned by just messing around with food, trying things out on unsuspecting friends, and watching the looks on their faces. Most of the guys on the teams—and the drivers for sure—don't cut you much slack if what they're eating tastes like a pair of old tires.

Over the years, I made more and more recipes that made folks roll back their eyes and ask for another helping. I found tiny farmers' markets with the best produce all across America. And I learned how to combine cooking with my other great pleasures, fishing and hunting. There's nothing quite like cooking food you've gone out and got yourself, combining it with fresh veggies from a local farm, and setting it in front of your friends.

Personally, I'm not sure the world really needs another cookbook from a hoity-toity chef whose kitchen cost more than most folks' houses. And most folks I know don't know where to buy (or how to say) foie gras, let alone spend 10 hours making food that'll be gone in 20 minutes. But they do like their friends, they all have a grill somewhere in the backyard, and they know that nothing beats a good meal with folks who make you laugh.

That's what my cookbook is about. So fire up the grill, pour yourself a beer, and get ready for some not-too-hard recipes that'll make your taste buds happy. And if you're ever at a NASCAR race, look for me. I'm probably somewhere in the garage, hoping that today's menu will bring 'em back again.

Big John

Table of Contents

The same thing applies to grilling. If you bring all the right gadgets and goodies when you tailgate or hit the infield, it will make your life easier. I know—many times I didn't have them, and let me tell you, it's better with this stuff!

Of course, you don't always need everything on the list, but my advice is to get a nice, big plastic bin and fill it with as many of these items as you can so you'll always have them when you're ready to roll. Here are some of the items you should bring.

- **Grill** (no-brainer!)
- **Extra propane tank.** Nothing's worse than watching the flame die on that big, thick steak!
- **Fire extinguisher** (another no-brainer!)
- **Grill tools: tongs, flipper, and grill brush.** Leave those fork things that come with your grilling tool set at home. They're the best way to wreck everything
- **Meat thermometer**
- **5-gallon jug of water** (wash your hands when handling food, duh!)
- **Small washbasin**
- **Washcloths and hand towels**
- **Dish soap**
- **Cutting boards**
- **Sharp knives and large serving spoons**
- **Plastic forks, knives, spoons**

- **Plastic plates and bowls** (they are more stable than paper products)
- **Paper plates and bowls** (they are easier for a quick cleanup)
- **Trash bags**
- **Ziploc bags of all sizes**
- **Plastic storage containers for leftovers**
- **Reynolds Wrap Release aluminum foil**
- **Foil roasting pans of all sizes**
- **Pots and frying pans**
- **Paper towels and napkins**
- **Olive oil, butter, and Pam cooking spray**
- **Barbecue sauces**
- **Salt, pepper, and your favorite seasonings**
- **Fresh garlic and onions**
- **Mustard, ketchup, and relish**
- **Beer** (so you can barter with a neighbor in case you left some stuff at home!)
- **Card tables to set your stuff on**
- **Camping chairs** (you want to be comfy while putting down a beer)
- **Oven mitts or work gloves** for handling hot stuff

✖✖✖✖✖✖✖ *Grilling Tips*

I've been grilling for a long time, and you can bet I've made my share of mistakes. Ever see an entire chicken go up in flames? Well, it might be funny to watch, but when you're the cook, it makes you madder than heck. Over the years, I've kept track of what works and what doesn't. Here's some of my best advice.

Choose the Right Grill

For the recipes in this book, I used a gas grill. For tailgating, I think gas is the best way to go. It is quick to get going and easy to maintain a constant temperature. Some of my recipes call for using the grill as an oven, and it is almost impossible to do that over charcoal. Charcoal gets cooler as it burns out, and that makes it tough to keep things just right. On the other hand, charcoal's one big advantage is flavor. The real question is ease of use versus taste. I'm pretty busy on a race weekend, so I prefer ease of use! Some grills come with a special bin where you can put wood chips to create that smoky flavor. I don't use 'em, but some folks swear by them. You'll need to decide for yourself. The key thing to look for in a gas grill, if you ask me, is to make sure that the grill has three flame bars under the grilling surface. Next be sure your grill has a side burner—it's a real lifesaver, and a number of the recipes in this book require one.

Breaking In the Gas Grill

Once the new grill is assembled, you need to season it. It's really very simple.

Soak a couple of paper towels in some good olive oil or canola oil and rub it all over the lower cooking surface. Then get all three burners going nice and hot. Sprinkle salt and a very generous amount of black pepper over that surface and reduce the heat to medium. Let it burn up for about 35 to 40 minutes. All done!

Know When You're Hot and When You're Not

After seasoning the grill, it's time to get to know its personality. I say that because I've found that every grill is just a bit different; each has its own unique hot spots and cold spots. It's important to know where they are to make sure your food always comes out just right.

To find out where they are, plan on making a bunch of burgers or chicken (invite some friends who won't freak out if some of the food is a little overcooked). Start by lighting the grill. Bring it up to smoking-hot, high temperature. Place the meat all across the lower surface and cut back the heat to medium-high or medium. The meat will want to stick, but don't worry; once it's cooked, it will "release." You'll find that some areas of the grill will cook faster than others, so pay attention to where they are! Move the food on the "hot spots" to the areas that aren't so hot and the food from the "cold spots" to the hot spots and let them finish cooking. Balance cooking between the two locations and everything will come out just right.

Like a charcoal grill, your gas grill can be a smoker. Some grills are equipped with a chamber to place your presoaked wood chips in to accomplish smoking. If yours doesn't have that option, a shallow stainless steel pan can help out. Place your presoaked hardwood chips in that pan. Remove the racks from the lower surface of the grill and set the pan on top of the lava rocks or the bars, then put the racks back into place. Quickly bring the grill up to temperature. Place your food on the lower surface, close the lid, and turn the heat down to medium or medium-low. Then let the smoke do the work.

Cooking Fish

Most fish is very delicate. If you just throw it on the grill, you'll wreck it. What I like to do is prepare a foil packet for the fish so it kind of bakes and steams all at once.

If I do a recipe where the fish needs to be grilled, I use the help of a flat porcelain tray with small holes in it. This way my fish won't stick, crumble, and fall through the grill racks. Tuna and swordfish can survive being right on the grill. Even so, try to handle them as little as possible.

Is That Done Yet?

Here's a simple trick I learned to figure out how to tell when meats are done. Make a loose fist. Press on the skin of your hand between the base of your thumb and index finger. It's kind of squishy, right? When you press your tongs into meat on the grill and it feels like that, it means the meat is still uncooked or very rare.

Now tighten up your fist just a little and press the same spot. It should be a little firmer now. Meat on the grill that feels like this is medium. I don't think you should cook good meats any longer than this.

Finally, make a tight fist and feel that area once more. It should feel totally firm. Meat on the grill that feels like this is well done. If you're cooking steak, venison backstrap, or lamb and it feels like this when you touch it with the tongs, I'd say you just ruined it and you might as well find the nearest trash bin and park it. But that's just my opinion.

Flame Outs

Keep a small squirt bottle of water near the grill. I don't care how good of a griller you are—you're gonna have a flare-up, and just a small squirt will help out here. Pork is gonna give you the worst trouble because of all the fat, but I have a way to combat flare-ups. Place the pork on heavy-duty nonstick foil, turn the edges up a little, and cradle that good pork fat juice. If some of it gets out and causes a flare-up, douse it with a small amount of water—not a lot or you will be waiting six months for your hair to grow back in. Once the fat on your grilled items crisps up, you'll be fine.

Keep Your Grill Clean and Covered

There are a lot of products out there for cleaning the grill. I like to burn it off after each use, so when I'm done grilling I crank up the fire to wide open and let 'er go. After a couple of minutes, I turn it off. Then I take a good long-bristled stainless or brass wire brush to it and scrub it down.

Empty all the catch cans and pans after three or four uses. Don't let them build up because that's where a nasty under-the-grill grease fire can happen, and then you're in trouble.

Most external surfaces will clean nicely with a biodegradable, food-friendly orange cleaner. Now that it is all clean and cooled down, get that cover on to keep the weather from doing damage to it.

Fuel

Always keep an extra tank of propane handy. If you don't need it, maybe the neighbor will.

Moving Your Grill

When moving your grill to and from the racetrack or tailgate location, place the grill in the truck behind the cab with the hinged side of the lid to the back of the cab and tie it in securely. I have seen countles numbers of grill lids lying alongside the highway; an extra minute would have saved the day.

A Few Last Words of Advice

Lots of folks use the upper grilling surface to keep grilled items warm, but if it's for more than a couple of minutes, don't do it. The reason is simple.

All the good juices that are inside of your grilled meats will begin to leak out and you'll be on the way to making jerky.

If you need to keep things warm for a while get a foil pan. Place your meats in there—go ahead and layer them. If you're keeping chicken warm, put a small amount of water in the pan right away. For pork, after slicing and accumulating those delicious juices, add some water. For ribeyes and steaks, cover the pan tightly with foil; now the meats are in sauna steam heaven. Put the whole pan on the upper grilling surface and keep the heat down. Things will stay perfect for hours. If you run out of warming surfaces, you can use the closed lid to the grill as an extra warming surface as long as it is flat.

For hot dog lovers, remember this—use the upper racks for your roasting. The bottom surfaces are way too hot and your dogs become burnt offerings.

The thermometer that came with the grill tells you the temperature inside the grill and in some cases is also a meat thermometer. Using the thermometer means you can use your grill like an oven.

I think a side burner on your grill is a must, but in the event you don't have one, the lower surface of the grill is fine for using skillets and saucepans.

Keeping your food cold is a must too. Ice, dry ice, and good-quality coolers are the key here.

If You Insist on Charcoal

If you're just not gonna use a gas grill, then I recommend one of those nice, big kettle-style charcoal grills. Be sure it has a lid. No lid and you're dead.

Once your new grill is assembled, you need to season it. It will cost you a small bag of charcoal, some oil, and salt and pepper. Place a self-starting bag of charcoal in the kettle and light it. While that's heating up, get some good-quality olive oil or canola oil, moisten a paper towel with the oil, and slick up the grilling rack. Once you don't smell any more of the lighter fluid coming off the coals, place the grill rack over the heat. Sprinkle some salt and

a generous amount of black pepper over the oiled rack and let it blacken up real good. Step back because the pepper dust will burn and get to your sinuses big time! Let it burn off, and now it's ready for a few years of good, solid grilling. Make sure to empty the coal dust after each grilling. Coal debris left in the grill is very caustic and shortens the life of your grill. Rust and corrosion are the enemies here. In other words, keep up with the upkeep!

Have a Smoke

Your charcoal grill is also a smoker. Use hardwood to smoke your main course of meat, chicken, or fish. Wet wood chips—apple, cherry, oak—are always favorites, but hickory is big as well. Lay the wet chips on the hot coals and place the grill rack on the grill. Place your meat on the grill and put the lid on with a small amount of draft. It will take a little longer cook the meat, chicken, or fish.

Hot and Cold

When you cook with charcoal, I think it's a good idea to be sure most of your coals are on one side of the kettle. This gives you a hot zone and a cool zone, so you can do direct and indirect cooking. For searing and fast grilling, place your meats right over the hot coals (direct cooking). For slow cooking, place your meats off to the side of the hot coals (indirect cooking). Plus, if you get a big flare-up going, you can rescue that meat by moving it away from the heat and into the cooler area.

Safety

Always keep a fire extinguisher nearby and a first-aid kit in the event of problems with the grill.

NEVER leave your grill unattended while you have food on the cooking surface. A fire can happen at any moment, and you need to be there to take care of business when it does! Also don't park your grill underneath an easy-up or awning connected to your RV. That's the first thing that will catch on fire when you have a flare-up. Safety is no accident here! A little rain isn't going to hurt your grill or the food inside it.

Good grilling!

The West

Sonoma & Fontana

The West Coast—mountains, beaches, fertile valleys, swimming pools, movie stars, a variety of fruits and nuts, and two terrific racetracks in California: Fontana and Sonoma.

Fontana has a superspeedway. It's one of two 2-mile tracks on the circuit offering up 3-wide racing, great weather, and the chance to spot a few Hollywood celebs. I won't lie to you—I'd use any excuse to get to Los Angeles—I'm a Dodgers fan. If they aren't in town I'll even drop in on Mickey and Goofy at Disneyland to watch the Angels.

Southern California's crazy cuisine is phenomenal and usually offers a few surprises, like the great little place that isn't there the next time you go looking for it. But there is a Thai place in fashionable Larchmont that you can count on. You'll find that more than the menu is a pleasure to behold. House of Chan Dara's waitresses are even hotter than the entrées.

One of only two road courses on the entire circuit is located in northern California's wine country. Sonoma is a great place to take in a road race. If you're lucky enough to get a spot on the southern hillside along turns 2 through 6, you can see almost the entire track from one position. That just doesn't happen anywhere else.

If you take a trip through the wineries, play it safe and designate a driver. Remember while touring to count the number of times someone will tell you, "Sonoma makes wine and NAPA makes auto parts!" Sure, I have an opinion; and Gundlach Bundschu is a winery to check out. They make some outstanding reds. I was once lucky enough to enjoy a red while I caught my boys in blue playing the Bay area's own Giants. The stars must have been aligned that night.

The food in northern California is completely different from East Coast fare. The seafood choices in the Bay area will have your head spinning faster than a Goodyear. Don't think that you have to go into the city to find the best places either. I'd never heard of petrale but I have never been one to shy away from anything. I ordered it with some barbecued oysters at Saylor's Landing in Sausalito and soon found out why that right-eyed flounder is a San Francisco favorite. Any place that can get away with misspelling its own name is all right in my book.

Need a Handout?

The garage area in Fontana has a great layout for the teams. Unlike a lot of tracks, they have power for the haulers, so it's oddly quiet with no generators running. One race day, Peter Rabbit, the driver of the 18 hauler, comes over to see me. He hints around, and I find out he didn't bring a grill. No problem. I was already making lunch for my three teams, so I whipped up my special pork loin roast and baked potatoes for everyone. Joe Gibbs asked where lunch came from, and Peter just kind of shrugged. I always say you should take care of your friends in the garage because you never know when you might need a favor in return!

This Little Piggy Pork Tenderloin

Serves 4 to 6

The tenderloin is a much smaller cut of meat with no fat, so make sure you read the labels correctly at the grocery store!

1 For the rub, mix together the thyme, rosemary, red basil, lemon-pepper, garlic powder, and onion powder. In a large mixing bowl combine water and juice of 2 lemons. Soak grape leaves in the lemon water for 10 minutes.

2 Take the pork tenderloins out of the package and rinse with water. Use paper towels to pat the tenderloins down until they are almost dry. Place the tenderloins on a cutting board and pour equal amounts of dry rub over each. Rub seasonings all over meat, coating evenly. Wrap each tenderloin in 6 grape leaves and use butcher's twine to secure.

3 Preheat grill to medium. Place pork on lower cooking surface, close lid, and reduce heat to medium low (275°F to 325°F). Cook, covered, until a meat thermometer reaches 140°F to 145°F, turning every 10 minutes to prevent burning. (This piece of meat doesn't have much fat, so slow and low-heat cooking works best.) Remove meat and let rest for 10 minutes on a clean cutting board.

4 Remove twine and grape leaves from meat. Slice tenderloins into ½-inch to ¼-inch medallions and serve.

4   tablespoons dried thyme*

4   tablespoons dried rosemary*

4   tablespoons dried basil*

4   tablespoons lemon-pepper

1   teaspoon garlic powder

1   tablespoon onion powder

2   cups water

2   lemons, juiced

12 grape leaves

2   pork tenderloins, 1 to 1½ pounds each

1   roll butcher's twine, soaked in water

*See Hint, page 33.

Second Place Is the First Loser

One year at Sonoma it looked like Sterling Marlin was gonna win his first road course race. It was getting down to the wire, and Jeff Gordon was in first and we were right behind him. Good thing was Jeff hadn't made a pit stop in ages and we could pretty much bet he wasn't going to make it on fuel. Well, it's a good thing we weren't in Vegas because we all called it wrong. Jeff made it in without stopping, and Sterling took second. Back home, all my friends were congratulating us on a great run. All I can say is we didn't travel 3,000 miles to finish second. That one really hurt.

1 Build the steak kabobs by alternating steak pieces, onion quarters, and mushroom caps on 4 steel skewers. On another set of 4 steel skewers build the chicken kabobs by alternating chicken pieces, bell peppers, and tomatoes.

2 In a mixing bowl combine olive oil and minced garlic. Mix thoroughly, then brush all sides of the prepared skewers with a light coat of oil. Season all sides of the beef kabobs with steak seasoning. Then season all sides of the chicken kabobs with chicken seasoning.

3 Preheat grill to medium-high. Place all of the skewers on the lower cooking surface and close lid. Reduce heat to medium and cook for 12 to 14 minutes or until chicken is no longer pink (170°F), turning often to keep from burning. When the chicken is done, remove the skewers from the grill and cover to keep warm. Continue cooking the beef skewers until they reach medium (160°F).

OPTIONAL: Brush the steak kabobs with your favorite steak sauce and the chicken kabobs with your favorite barbecue sauce to jazz things up!

2	pounds boneless New York strip steaks, cut into 1-inch pieces
1	large sweet onion, quartered
8	ounces mushrooms, stems removed
2	pounds boneless, skinless chicken breast halves, cut into 1-inch pieces
2	yellow bell peppers, seeded, cut into 1½-inch squares
8	ounces cherry tomatoes
1	cup olive oil
4	cloves garlic, minced
	McCormick Montreal steak seasoning
	McCormick Montreal chicken seasoning

What Deer?

While at Sonoma I was shooting the bull with Dick Trickle about hunting when we begin talking about guns, and he starts rambling about how he likes his 280 Winchester. I look up the hill next to the track and see some deer munching on lunch at the top. So I ask Dick if he could hit the deer at the top of the hill with his 280. He starts going on and on again about how he did this and that, so I finally had to repeat the question. Dick finally says, "Yeah, I could nail them." I tell ya, if Dick spent as much time on the car as he did talking about hunting, he might have won a few more races!

LA LA LA Chicken Pizza Serves 4

This is a perfect dish to prepare after making Speedway Chicken because you can use up the leftovers (if you have any) on the pizza!

1 Use a good pizza stone that will fit in the grill for this recipe. Rub the pizza stone with olive oil and sprinkle with cornmeal. Place crust on the stone.

2 Use the back of a spoon to evenly spread out the barbecue sauce on the crust. Place the chicken pieces evenly over the sauce and sprinkle the onion on top. Finish by sprinkling cheese evenly over the onions.

3 Preheat grill to 350°F to 375°F. Place stone in the center of the grill and bake with lid closed for 15 to 20 minutes. Rotate stone once during baking to make sure pizza cooks evenly. The pizza is done when the edge of the crust is golden brown and the sauce and cheese are slightly bubbling in the middle.

HINT: Preheating the pizza stone on the grill will make a crisper crust.

1	premade pizza crust (such as Boboli)
1	tablespoon olive oil
¼	cup cornmeal
½	cup Sweet Baby Ray's barbecue sauce
2	chicken breasts, leftover from Speedway Chicken Sandwiches (page 27), cut into ½-inch to ¾-inch cubes
½	red onion, chopped
16	ounces shredded 4-cheese pizza blend

Can I See Some ID?

One day the 42 team and I decide to go out to dinner. We get there and find out the wait is two hours. Well, I schmooze the manager and get us a table in 15 minutes. Then Kyle Petty walks in with Stephen Mofit, so I pull some chairs from the table next to us. This ticks off the manager. I explain, "I'm just getting a chair for Kyle here." The manager says, "I know who Kyle Petty is, and that's not him. If that's Petty, I'll buy you dinner." Kyle pulls out all his IDs, and the guy still insists he isn't Kyle. Finally some fans at the bar back us up. I'll give that manager credit; he stuck to his word and picked up the tab.

1 In a mixing bowl combine olive oil, black pepper, garlic, chicken seasoning, lemon-pepper, Worcestershire sauce, mustard, barbecue sauce, and Italian dressing. Mix thoroughly, then pour into a 1-gallon resealable bag. Place chicken in the bag and squish to coat. Marinate in the cooler for up to 4 hours.

2 Preheat grill to medium-high. Place chicken on lower cooking surface; close lid and reduce heat to medium. Cook chicken for 6 to 7 minutes on each side or until centers are juicy and hot and a meat thermometer reaches 170°F. The last couple of minutes cooking, put cheese slices on chicken to melt and place the buns split sides down on the upper cooking surface to toast.

3 Butter buns and build sandwiches with the tomato slices, lettuce, mayonnaise, and the hot and tasty chicken.

HINT: Coleslaw also tastes great on these sandwiches.

¼	cup extra virgin olive oil
1	tablespoon black pepper
2	teaspoons garlic, minced
1	teaspoon McCormick herb chicken seasoning
1	teaspoon lemon-pepper
1	tablespoon Worcestershire sauce
1	tablespoon yellow mustard
2–3	tablespoons barbecue sauce (your favorite)
¼	cup zesty Italian dressing
8	boneless, skinless chicken breast halves
8	slices extra-sharp provolone cheese
8	poppy seed buns
¼	cup butter, softened
2	tomatoes, sliced
8	iceberg lettuce leaves Mayonnaise

My Hard Card

One of the grocery store chains I shop at out West is Safeway. Well, to save the team a little money, I signed up for Safeway's Club Card, which is red and looks like the old Winston Cup credential. I did my shopping and went back to the track in Sonoma to make the boys lunch. To get in the garage, you have to show your hard card or credential. Without thinking, I grab my Safeway card, flash it to the guards at the gate, and walk in like I own the place. It took 'em a second, but sure enough, they caught up with me pretty fast! Good thing I had the real hard card, or no one was going to eat that day!

Greens with Poppy Seed Dressing
Serves 4 to 6

You can mix your own greens or buy them prepackaged.

1 In a stainless-steel mixing bowl combine the spring mix, onion, tomato, and carrot. Cover with plastic wrap and place in cooler or refrigerator to chill.

2 In a blender combine the sugar, vinegar, poppy seeds, grated onion, salt, and dry mustard. Blend at medium speed while slowly adding salad oil in a steady stream until reaching desired consistency. Store in a tightly covered sealable container. Chill until ready to use.

3 When ready to serve, stir up dressing and drizzle over greens in bowl. Toss salad to evenly coat.

HINT: You can prepare both items at home and bring them to the track ready to go!

1	16-ounce package spring salad mix
¼	red onion, finely diced
1	large tomato, seeded and finely chopped
1	carrot, peeled and shredded
½	cup sugar
⅓	cup cider vinegar
1	tablespoon poppy seeds
1	tablespoon grated onion
1	teaspoon salt
1	teaspoon dry mustard
1	cup salad oil

Take Me Out to a Ball Game

The spotter for driver Greg Biffle is a guy named Joel Edmund. Joel used to be the batboy for Dodgers manager Tommy Lasorda. I'm a die-hard Dodgers fan, so when I found this out, of course I had to lean on him to hook me up with some Dodger tickets. One year while we were at a race in Sonoma, the Dodgers were playing the Giants in San Francisco at Candlestick. Joel gives Tommy a call and he pulls some strings. The seats we got were almost on the field. Not only was I in heaven, my boys in blue won the game too! I felt like I dang near won the lottery.

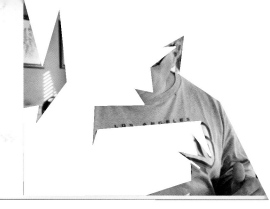

1 Take 4 steel skewers and build kabobs by alternating pineapple, apples, pears, bananas, and cherries. Brush a light coat of canola oil on all sides of the fruit on skewers.

2 Preheat grill to medium-high. Place skewers on lower cooking surface. Close lid and cook, turning frequently, for 6 to 8 minutes. Remove and place on a serving plate. Dust kabobs lightly with powdered sugar.

1   fresh pineapple, crown removed, peeled, cored, and cut into 1-inch pieces

4   Gala apples, cored and cut into 1-inch pieces

4   pears, cored and cut into 1-inch pieces

4   bananas, peeled, sliced, and cut into 1½-inch pieces

1   8-ounce jar maraschino cherries

1   cup canola oil

Powdered sugar

She Done Blowed Up

Henry Benfield works as the motor coach driver for the MB2/MBV Motorsports team. One time in Sonoma I saw him by Ken Schrader's rental car. Now, Henry's quite the prankster, so I had to see what's going down. Henry's got the grille of the rental completely taped shut with clear packing tape. Henry's busting up because he's also put a thin layer of grease on the windshield wiper. After the race, Ken gets in the car and heads to the airport. Sure enough, the car overheats and blows up in traffic. Ken hits the wipers and smears the grease all over the windshield and can't see anything. I hear he ended up thumbing it to the airport. The secret's out, Henry!

Topanga Surprise Grilled Veggies

Serves 4 to 6

Grilling veggies for a side dish is quick, easy, and tastes great. You can choose your favorites or go with mine.

1 Preheat grill to medium-high. Clean grill thoroughly with a steel brush. With a basting brush or towel, coat the grill lightly with some of the olive oil.

2 Place all of the veggies in a foil pan and coat with olive oil. Remove from foil pan (save the oil) and lay vegetables on the grill's lower cooking surface. Grill for about 6 minutes per side with the lid closed. Make sure to not overcook the vegetables; they should have a little crispness to them. Remove and place on a serving tray or in a foil roasting pan.

3 In a bowl whisk the balsamic vinegar into the remaining olive oil, mixing until it is almost an emulsion. Drizzle the dressing over the vegetables. Finish by lightly seasoning with the salt and white pepper.

HINT: As long as we're using fresh veggies in this recipe, let's talk about fresh herbs. I grow my own herbs, put them in bundles, and hang them up to dry. This means that I get the best flavors when I cook. If you're using store-bought dried herbs, you can't let them sit around in your cabinet for years. If you haven't used them in six months, throw them away because they will have lost their flavor.

1	cup olive oil
2	eggplants, cut into 3/8-inch-thick rings
4	carrots, peeled and sliced in half lengthwise
2	yellow bell peppers, seeded and cut lengthwise into quarters
2	red bell peppers, seeded and cut lengthwise into quarters
4	green zucchini squash, cut in half lengthwise
4	yellow zucchini squash, cut in half lengthwise
2	bunches green onions
2	teaspoons balsamic vinegar
	Sea salt
	Ground white pepper

Kabobs or Kaboom?

My first race at Fontana had some unexpected excitement. During the national anthem they had a fly-by with some Air Force jets. But this time, one of the jets was flying at supersonic speed and set off a gigantic sonic boom. I was back at the hauler cleaning up some stuff, and Mrs. Sabates, the team owner's wife, was with me and about to have a smoke. When the boom hit, the doors to the hauler rattled so much I thought they'd fall off. Then I saw Mrs. Sabates, and she must have tried to light up right when the boom hit because she dropped that cigarette like it caused the noise! Maybe that's what got her to quit?

Yippee Aïoli Potato Salad
Serves 6 to 8

This garlicky recipe is easy to make before you head to the track. Bring breath mints!

1 On the side burner of your grill boil potatoes until they are almost cooked through. Don't overcook them or they will turn to mush in the salad. Drain and allow to cool. Once cool, cut the potatoes into 1/2-inch cubes.

2 Preheat the grill to 325°F. Cut the tops off the garlic heads, exposing the fresh garlic. Drizzle olive oil over the top and put a pinch of salt on top. Wrap the garlic in aluminum foil and place on lower cooking surface of grill. Bake with lid closed for 45 to 60 minutes. Check periodically to make sure you don't overcook the garlic.

3 To make the aïoli place mayonnaise in a blender. Squeeze the roasted garlic from skins into the blender. Add the minced garlic, garlic salt, and the salt and black pepper to taste. Blend thoroughly. You can hand mix this in a stainless steel bowl with a whisk if a blender is not available.

4 In a large resealable plastic bag mix the potatoes, celery, onion, carrot, peas, and celery seeds. Mix in the aïoli by kneading the bag gently, coating all the vegetables. Season to taste with sea salt and white pepper.

2	pounds new potatoes, peeled
2	heads fresh garlic
1/4	cup olive oil
1 1/2	cups mayonnaise
1	tablespoon minced garlic
1/4	teaspoon garlic salt
	Salt
	Black pepper
3	10-inch celery stalks, finely diced
1/2	cup Vidalia onion, finely diced (may substitute any sweet onion)
1	carrot, shredded
1/4	pound snap peas, pods removed
2	teaspoons celery seeds
	Sea salt
	Ground white pepper

The Southwest
Phoenix & Las Vegas

The desert Southwest—sun, sand, wind, cactus, danger, and a really big ditch (that'd be the Grand Canyon). Oh, and a couple of racetracks too. Anything that lives here has evolved to grow spines or poisons to stay alive. It has an odd effect on drivers as well.

The racetrack at Las Vegas can be credited for the term "cookie cutter." It's designed in similar fashion to many of the 1½-mile tri-ovals on the stock car circuit. If it worked once … why not? My money is on a UFO from Area 51 leading a single-file freight train rollin' at 165 mph after about 50 laps. On second thought, maybe I'll go with the return of "The King," and I'm not talkin' about Richard Petty.

Vegas typically finds its fans hanging out on the Strip and not in the parking lots. You can watch it all from the outside balcony of the Ghost Bar at the top of the Palms Casino. It's got an all-glass floor—you'd think someone left their windshield there. You can walk right out on it and look straight down. Don't worry, you won't fall through, but it kind of freaks you out. With all the casinos, the fine dining opportunities are endless. But if you're looking for something quick, cheap, and good, you gotta go to In-N-Out Burger and muscle a double-double with grilled onions.

The Phoenix International Raceway in Arizona has

a one-of-a-kind shape: a mile oval with a dogleg on the backstretch. Racing at Phoenix is always side-by-side with a lot of action (and a few cautions) coming out of turn 2. I'll never forget the time John Andretti stuck the No. 43 into the STP sign in turn 4, which just so happens was his sponsor. Talk about lining up that advertising dollar for an hour of red-flag of repair.

The fans at PIR turn the parking lot into their own sin city! For the right amount of cash you can get your RV inside the track. If you're on a budget, the parking lot in the outfield is the way to go. Heck, they even build a temporary grocery store under a giant tent just in case you run out of anything.

I love going to the races in the Southwest because the food is so different from the stuff I get at home in Pennsylvania—especially the Mexican food selections. I've been to a variety of Mexican restaurants, and the cuisine is a big influence in my recipes for this region. Not all peppers are the same. The flavors can be subtle and the heat varies greatly. You might consider wearing rubber gloves when handling chili peppers—and don't rub your eyes.

And speaking of heat—hey, it's Phoenix—it's hot. If I had a dollar for every time I've heard "It's a dry heat," I could afford my own race team and have them cook for me.

It's Not a Fish Story!

One season we caught a couple of nice trout at Big Lake in eastern Arizona. The morning of the race, I get the grill out and soon the crew guys come over to mooch. I hold out this beautiful trout, and this gets the attention of Ken Schrader, whose rig is parked next door. Ken asks me where I caught the fish. I show him some pictures of the lake, and one shot looks like I'm standing in piles of snow. He asks me how deep it was and I tell him, "All I know is I jumped in and sank to my armpits!" I never told him that it only snowed three inches and I was next to a drift.

Soft as a Flat Burrito Wraps
Serves 8 to 10

I prefer to use Arizona brand flour tortillas, but you can try flavored tortillas too, which can spice things up.

1 Lay out all ingredients on a table in an assembly line.

2 Spread cream cheese on one side of the flour tortilla.

3 Sprinkle shredded cheese on top of cream cheese. Place spinach over shredded cheese. Sprinkle onion and green chilies over spinach.

4 Top onion and green chilies with ham. Roll up tortillas and slice into 1-inch-thick pieces. Arrange on a serving plate and dig in!

- 2   8-ounce packages cream cheese, softened
- 10   10-inch Arizona flour tortillas
- 16   ounces shredded Mexican 4-cheese blend
- 1   bunch fresh spinach, stems removed
- 1   medium red onion, finely diced
- 6   medium hot whole roasted green chilies, peeled, seeded, & diced (or substitute two 4-ounce cans of medium hot diced green chilies)
- 16   ounces thinly sliced deli ham

The Real Deal in New Mexican Food

When you're at a race in Phoenix, check out some of the local restaurants to experience some real Southwest cooking. There's a place called Los Dos Molinos that serves up some of the hottest New Mexican food in town. The signature dish to get is the adovada ribs. This will get your forehead sweating and your nose runnin', but man, is it worth it! About the only cool things on the menu are the cheese crisp and the carnitas, so be warned! Most of the dishes on the menu are at least a two-cerveza affair, so kick back and enjoy a good sweat!

It Ain't Chilie Here Cheeseburgers Serves 8

Anybody can grill a burger. But to make a great burger, you need to get a little creative!

1 In a large bowl mix ground beef, onion, red and green bell peppers, canned green chilies, eggs, bread crumbs, black pepper, and garlic. Shape mixture into eight ¾-inch-thick patties. Preheat the grill to medium-high. Place the burgers on the lower cooking surface and cook with the lid closed for 14 to 18 minutes or until done (160°F), turning burgers frequently to prevent burning.

2 Top burgers with a whole roasted green chile and a slice of Monterey Jack cheese during the last 1 minute of grilling. Meanwhile, on the upper cooking surface place split buns facedown. Close the lid and continue to cook until the cheese is melted and the buns are toasted.

3 Serve with your favorite condiments.

4 pounds 90 percent lean ground beef

1 yellow onion, finely diced

1 small red bell pepper, seeded and finely diced

1 small green bell pepper, seeded and finely diced

2 4-ounce cans green chilies

3 large eggs

1 cup Italian-style bread crumbs

1 tablespoon black pepper

4 cloves garlic, minced

8 whole roasted medium green chilies, peeled and seeded

8 slices Monterey Jack cheese

8 potato buns

   Assorted condiments

Dungaree Doll

At the inaugural race at Las Vegas, Mrs. Sabates, my team owner's wife, surprised me with 60 starving guests. Luckily I had a ton of meat, so I borrowed a grill and went into overdrive. Right then Paula Marlin, Sterling Marlin's wife, walks by in a killer suit and says, "Hey, Big John, you need some help?" I'm like, "I'll take any help I can get!" She grabs a knife and hits the onions. Mrs. Sabates comes back and almost has a heart attack seeing Paula. "What are you doing cutting onions in that gorgeous suit?" she asks. Paula replies, "I cut onions every weekend, whether it's in dungarees or this." Paula gives Mrs. Sabates a hug, and we pull off lunch without a hitch.

Aunt Sue's Sloppy Joes
Serves 8

You might want to wear some of your older racing garb when eating this stuff. It usually gets all over the place.

1 In a large skillet on the side burner melt butter and cook onion over medium heat until translucent.

2 Add the ground beef and cook until brown. Add the remaining ingredients (except the buns) one at a time and mix well.

3 Reduce heat to medium-low and cook, covered, for about 20 minutes. Spoon onto buns and serve with tons of napkins.

NOTE: For a sweeter taste, this recipe can be altered by using brown sugar in place of white sugar and adding 2 tablespoons of sweet pickle relish.

3	tablespoons butter
1	onion, diced
2	pounds 80 percent lean ground beef
1	8-ounce jar Heinz chili sauce
3	tablespoons ketchup
3	tablespoons yellow mustard
3	tablespoons sugar
3	tablespoons white vinegar
2	teaspoons salt
1½	teaspoons black pepper
8	large onion buns

Camping at the Ritz

One year I brought Bill Henderson, a crew member with Sabco, fishing with me. After a few days out, we looked pretty scraggly. We drove straight to the Ritz-Carlton. Bill and I made our way to the front desk, fishing poles, sleeping bags, and all. I knew we had reservations, but I couldn't help but ask the lady if they had any rooms. She looks us up and down and says they're all booked up! I say, "That's OK. We'll just roll out our stuff in the living room and wait for one!" She's totally speechless. At this point Bill ruins the joke and says, "We're with Team Sabco. You have a reservation for us." The look on her face was priceless!

Dan's Deep-Fried Quail Breasts

Serves 4

The key to this recipe is bagging enough quail to feed more than your pet Chihuahua. You can substitute chicken tenders.

1 Debone each quail breast and split into 2 separate pieces. In a bowl mix olive oil, garlic, and pepper. Add the breast halves and coat generously. Pour into a 1-gallon resealable plastic bag and place in refrigerator for up to 3 days.

2 Combine the herb chicken seasoning with the flour in a mixing bowl. Whisk eggs in another mixing bowl.

3 Cut a small hole in the bag of chips and press all the air out. Using a rolling pin on a cutting board, crush the chips to a fine crumb. Pour crushed chips into a third mixing bowl.

4 Fill deep fryer with oil and heat to 375°F. Coat the breasts in the flour mixture, then dip them in the egg wash. Next coat with the crushed chips. Place in pan or on a plate.

5 Remove fryer basket from deep fryer and fill with as many breasts as possible. Lower basket carefully into oil and cook until golden brown or until they begin to float. Repeat process until all breasts are done. Place cooked breasts on a plate lined with paper towels to drain.

20	whole quail breasts
1½	cups olive oil
5	cloves garlic, minced
4	tablespoons black pepper
4	tablespoons McCormick herb chicken seasoning
2	cups flour
6	large eggs
1	28-ounce bag French Onion Sun Chips
1	gallon peanut oil or canola oil

Did You Lose or Is It the Soup?

One time we had a postrace cookout at my buddy Eric's house in Phoenix. A friend of ours brings over former Busch Series champ David Green. So I'm grillin' up some chicken and burgers and Eric whips up a test concoction of what has become the soup recipe below. The only problem is that Eric used the wrong kind of chilies. He used those teeny ones that are so hot they peel the paint off the wall. Before anyone could stop him, David grabs a big bowl and digs in. In seconds he's got so many tears in his eyes we don't know if it's because he didn't win the race or the soup was too hot!

No Cryin' Green Chilie Soup

Serves 6 to 8

Farmers adjust the temperature of chilies by how much they water them. The smaller the amount of water, the hotter they get!

1 In a large soup pot combine the chicken broth, onion, potatoes, green chilies, garlic, bay leaves, oregano, pepper, salt, and hot pepper sauce. Place on the side burner of your grill; bring pot up to a boil for 2 to 3 minutes, then lower to a simmer. Cook, covered, until potatoes are tender. Add butter and stir until melted. Add the cream and simmer for 10 to 15 minutes.

2 Meanwhile preheat grill to medium-high. Season chicken with chicken seasoning and cook on grill, uncovered, for 12 to 15 minutes until chicken is no longer pink (170°F), turning once halfway through grilling. Remove chicken from grill and cut into 1/2-inch pieces.

3 Scoop the bay leaves out of the soup with a spoon and discard. Pour the soup into a blender or food processor and puree. Pour soup back into pot and add the cut-up chicken. Simmer soup for another 10 to 15 minutes to thicken.

4 Pour soup into bowls and top with shredded cheese.

Hint: See page 49 for how to roast your own chilies.

2	14-ounce cans chicken broth
1	onion, diced
2	large baking potatoes, peeled and diced
6	roasted green chilies (medium), peeled, seeded, and diced
3	cloves garlic, minced
4	bay leaves
1	tablespoon dried Mexican oregano
1	tablespoon black pepper
	Salt
1	tablespoon Louisiana hot sauce
1/4	cup butter
1/2	pint heavy whipping cream
3	large boneless, skinless chicken breasts
	Mrs. Dash chicken seasoning
8	ounces shredded Co-Jack cheese

A Hitchhiker's Guide to Manners

One year Sterling Marlin decided to take the scenic route to Arizona and rode with the team's truck driver. Of course the truck breaks down, and Sterling has an autograph session he can't miss. So he stands on the side of the road and sticks his thumb out. In no time an old sedan pulls over. The driver, an older woman, says, "Get in." Before he can thank her, she adds, "Behave yourself, young man, and you'll get to your destination." All Sterling could say was, "Yes, ma'am." Outside of Tucson, Sterling spots a competitor's rig and the lady drops him off. He made it to his session on time and got a lesson in manners too!

Bean There, Done That
Serves 6 to 8

You can buy canned green chilies, but nothing beats fresh, fire-roasted ones. The type we use are called Anaheims.

1 Preheat skillet on side burner to medium-high. Pour olive oil in skillet and add butter. Once butter is melted, lower heat to medium and place onion and bell peppers in pan. Saute onion and bell peppers for 10 minutes, then stir in green chilies and hot pepper sauce.

2 Add black beans to the skillet mixture. Add salt and black pepper to taste. Stir frequently until warm all the way through. Reduce to low heat, cover, and cook for 30 minutes to let the flavors blend. Stir occasionally to keep the beans from sticking to the pan.

Hint: To roast your own chilies, place whole chilies on grill on medium-high heat. Blacken both sides. Put blackened chilies into a paper bag and close bag. Let sit for 5 minutes. Take out of bag and peel off blackened skins. Delicious!

2	tablespoons olive oil
2	tablespoons butter
1	onion, diced
1	cup diced red bell peppers
1/2	cup diced roasted green Anaheim chilies (or substitute two 4-ounce cans of medium hot diced green chilies)
1	tablespoon Louisiana hot sauce
3	16-ounce cans Bush's black beans, drained
	Salt
	Black pepper

49

I Tried to Tell You

One fall I brought my brother-in-law Keith to Arizona to see the race and to do a little hunting. We're in the desert and I'm showing Keith the ropes. We come across a huge barrel cactus, and I tell Keith, "Whatever you do, don't kick or run into one of these." A moment later I think I hear a girl screaming, using language I can't repeat. I rush over to help, and it's no girl, it's Keith. He looks like a stuck pig with a spike in his toe. He tells me, "I kicked one." That spine must have penetrated almost an inch. Just like a 4-year-old—tell 'em not to touch something and what do they do?

So Hot It's Cool
Corn Salad
Serves 6 to 8

There's nothing like a little spicy cool when hanging out in the Southwest. No grillin' needed for this treat!

1 In a plastic mixing bowl combine the corn and other vegetables together along with the garlic and cilantro. Squeeze the lemon over veggies and mix.

2 In another bowl combine the hot sauce and the balsamic vinegar. Whisk in the olive oil in a slow steady stream; stop just short of making an emulsion. Throw a couple of pinches of Cajun spice in the mix and blend it in.

3 Pour dressing over corn mixture and fold in with spoon. Cover with plastic wrap and chill for at least 2 hours. Stir mixture again before serving.

1	11-ounce can white shoe peg corn, undrained
1	11-ounce can yellow corn
½	red onion, finely diced
1	red bell pepper, finely diced
2	radishes, finely diced
1	clove garlic, minced
¼	cup loosely packed fresh cilantro leaves, chopped
½	lemon
1½	tablespoons Louisiana hot sauce
4	tablespoons balsamic vinegar
½	cup olive oil
2	pinches salt-free Cajun spice

Beer Spinning

Nothing beats an ice-cold beer when it's hot. But what do you do when you run out of cold ones? Here's a trick I taught Sterling Marlin years ago, and it'll get you a frosty one in no time. First dump a bag of ice into the cooler for those other beers. Next put one beer into a small plastic bag or bucket and add a few handfuls of ice until the can is almost covered. Spin the can for two minutes. Pop it and aaaah, ice cold! To get the beers in the cooler cold, add some water so the beers bob around just a bit—they'll be perfectly chilled in less than 10 minutes. And yeah, it works for soda pop too.

Around the Track Onion Rings
Serves 6

This recipe will dip into your beer stash, but makes good rings great! Serve 'em up hot from the fryer and watch 'em disappear.

1 Slice onions into rings, ½ inch to ¾ inch thick. Prepare the batter by mixing flour and beer in a large mixing bowl. Blend well and let stand 3 hours. Make sure sliced onions are dry.

2 Heat canola oil in a deep fryer to 360°F to 365°F. With a fork, batter slices of 1 onion and drop in the deep fryer one ring at a time. Cook until golden brown or until the rings float. Remove with basket and place on a plate covered with paper towels to drain. Repeat process for the rest of the onions. Season with salt and pepper to taste.

HINT: You can use a wok on the side burner if you don't have a deep fryer.

6   large yellow onions

5   cups self-rising flour

3   12-ounce cans beer
     (I like Newcastle for this)

1   gallon canola oil
     Salt
     Black pepper

Never Race an Expert

Coors Light sponsored our team for the first time in 1995, and they even set up a private game room in Phoenix. After qualifying, we all went to check it out. One of the arcade games was a two-person racetrack with side-by-side seats. Kyle Petty hops in and asks, "Who's gonna race me?" The guys just sit there twiddling their thumbs, so I step up to the plate. Kyle and me go at it, and I'm leading into the last lap. Kyle turns to me and says, "I'll fix you!" The next thing I know, Kyle's car hits me head on! He's laughing his head off—he spun his car around and drove it backward to crash into me!

When You Get Lemons Lemonade

Serves 4 to 6

Freeze the concentrate, then thaw it out for your next party!

1 Cut the ends off of two of the lemons and cut each lemon into quarters. Blend lemons (including the peel), sugar, and 2 cups water in blender on puree. Strain and add the juice of one more lemon. You can freeze this concentrate for future use or combine with 5 more cups of water and serve over ice. Garnish with a lemon slice.

NOTE: You can also bring a bottle of your favorite vodka and mix into the lemonade to taste—but only those of you who are over 21!

3	large lemons
1½	cups sugar
7	cups water
	Ice cubes
1	lemon, sliced

Barbecue Country

Texas & Kansas

I love barbecue country: 10-gallon hats, cowboy boots, longhorns, oil wells, big red barns, wide open spaces, tornadoes, two-steppin', and a couple of really fast racetracks.

Just to set the record straight, Texas Motor Speedway is in Fort Worth, not Dallas. Seems the folks over at the Fort Worth Chamber of Commerce got their panties in a wad over all the TV commentators saying they're in Dallas. Must be some kind of sibling rivalry.

It took a few tries to get this track paved right for the drivers, and now it is one fast hombré. One of the most unusual things at the track is in the infield near the garage area. The food court sits on these pavers that are in the shape of Texas. The crazy thing is that they all interlock. I'm still trying to figure that one out!

Since I tend to follow history a little bit, on one of my race weekends I had to visit Dealey Plaza in Dallas, where JFK was killed. It was kind of creepy. There was almost nobody around, and I'd have to say there's a weird aura about the place. Within minutes I needed a change of pace, so I beat a hasty retreat just north of Fort Worth for a meal at Fresco's Cocina, a Mexican place. They make a smooth sangria swirl margarita.

Kansas is a macaroon on the cookie cutter chart! The speedway looks like an F5 tornado hit Las Vegas, picked up the track, and dropped it on the Kansas countryside, minus the ruby slippers and a dog named Toto! Kansas Speedway officially opened in 2001, hosting its first Cup race just in time for the storm season.

I almost wish a Vegas-style casino had blown in with that same F5 to provide a cheap buffet! You could wander west to Lawrence and do just fine, but Kansas City has a lot going on. Crawl from pub to pub in the historic and laid-back Westport district. This little area is wall-to-wall with live music, restaurants, and shops, and it knows how to have a good time. Just down the hill is the elegant Country Club Plaza. You'll need a clean pair of sneakers. I think there must be more fountains in KC than in Paris, France, or Paris, Texas, for that matter. And if you can't find it at the City Market down by the river, you weren't really looking. This open-air market has been running seven days a week since 1857. Of course, back then you might have been wrestling for rutabaga with the likes of Doc Holliday and Jesse James.

X Marks the Spot

Cooking times for meat vary, and it's usually related to the thickness of the meat. If you're grilling a pork loin as a roast, especially a whole loin, you'll need about 10 to 12 minutes a pound, so plan on being there for about an hour and turn the roast occasionally. For steaks about ¾ inch thick, try about 5 to 7 minutes a side. For the first side, put your steak on the hot grill for 2 to 3 minutes and don't touch it. Then pick it up and rotate it 90 degrees and set it back down on an unused part of the grill (it's hotter). This will give you nice XX grill marks. After another 3 to 4 minutes, flip it and do the same thing.

I Want My Baby Back Ribs
Serves 6 to 8

This recipe will also work with St. Louis-style pork ribs. But I prefer baby back ribs.

1 Use a steel shish kabob skewer to remove the membrane on the back side of the ribs. To do this, slide the point between the membrane and meat and slowly lift up. Grab the membrane with your fingers and peel away from the ribs. Cut each rack of ribs in half.

2 To make the rub, mix together paprika, brown sugar, pepper, and salt. On a large cutting board, lay out the ribs and generously pour rub all over both sides of the ribs. Use 4 foil roasting pans and double them up for rigidity so you have a total of 2 pans. Place 6 half racks of ribs in each pan. Sprinkle onion and garlic over each half rack of ribs. Cover pans with aluminum foil.

3 Preheat grill to 300°F. Place both pans on the lower cooking surface. Close lid on grill and roast for 2 to 2½ hours. Check ribs every half hour after the first hour of baking. Spoon juices over ribs when you open the foil to check their progress. Remove pans and let ribs rest, uncovered, for 10 minutes.

4 Turn grill up to medium. Place ribs, bone sides down, on lower cooking surface. Turn ribs as needed (every 5 to 7 minutes). Cook for an additional 30 minutes. At the end, baste both sides with barbecue sauce and cook for 5 minutes.

6	full racks baby back ribs
½	cup paprika
½	cup brown sugar, packed
½	cup black pepper
¼	cup kosher salt
1	large yellow onion, diced
6	cloves garlic, minced
1	18-ounce bottle Sweet Baby Ray's barbecue sauce

Not a Whole Row

Jimmy Spencer's sister, Chris, is always full of fun stories. One day during a rain delay, Chris starts telling me a story about when she and Jimmy were kids. They built an old junker of a car in their parents' auto wrecking yard, and Chris got the crazy idea of opening up the doors on a whole row of wrecked cars. Then she and Jimmy took their junker and plowed through them. Chris went on to say, "My mom would kill me if she ever found out." Well, hello, Mrs. Spencer! She followed Chris around the garage in Pocono for two days mumbling, "A whole row, I can't believe a whole row!" I don't think Chris will ever tell me a story again!

To a T-Bone Steaks
Serves 6

You know, sometimes taking the easy way out makes the most sense. This is a real simple way to make great steaks!

1 Place two steaks each in one-gallon resealable plastic bags. Pour equal amounts of steak grilling sauce in each bag. Seal bags and shake to cover meat evenly. Marinate for 4 hours in your cooler or refrigerator.

2 Heat grill to medium-high. Place steaks on lower cooking surface and close lid. Turn heat down to medium. After 4 minutes lift up steaks and rotate 90 degrees on same side. After 4 more minutes flip steaks over. Rotate again 90 degrees on second side after another 4 minutes. The steak should be cooked to medium at this point (160°F). Adjust cooking time to desired degree of doneness.

3 While cooking steaks, place a large skillet on the side burner and heat to medium-high. Add olive oil and butter. Stir in onions and sugar and cook until onions take on some color (about 15 minutes). Add mushrooms and season with salt, pepper, and hot sauce (if desired) to taste. The mushrooms are done when they take on some color and are semi-firm.

4 Serve steaks with cooked onions and mushrooms on top.

6	T-bone steaks (12–16 ounces each)
1	14-ounce bottle McCormick Montreal steak grilling sauce
2	tablespoons extra-virgin olive oil
1/4	cup butter
2	yellow onions, peeled and sliced
1	tablespoon sugar
1	pound button mushrooms
	Salt
	Black pepper
	Louisiana hot sauce (optional)

This Isn't Really Our Lunch, Is It?

Back in the early days, the racing teams didn't do much to take care of the crew. We were lucky to have a package of bologna, some cheese, and a crushed loaf of bread in the cooler for lunch. My team owner at the time, James Hylton, would take care of us at dinnertime by taking us out to a local restaurant. I usually would grab some track food to hold me over until then. Years of lousy sandwich fixings finally pushed me over the edge. When I worked for Team Sabco, I finally broke down and got one of the truck drivers to bring me a grill. The rest is history.

No Bull Turkey Burgers Serves 4

The secret to a great turkey burger is to make sure that one-third of the ground turkey is dark meat.

1 In a large bowl mix ground turkey, poultry seasoning, and pepper. Form into 4 half-pound patties.

2 Preheat grill to medium-high. Place patties on lower cooking surface. Close lid and reduce heat to medium. Cook 5 to 7 minutes on each side. To check if the burgers are done, use a meat thermometer and make sure the centers are 155°F to 160°F.

3 Once the burgers come to desired temperature, salt to taste and place cheese on top. Meanwhile, split kaiser rolls and place facedown on upper cooking surface. Close lid and cook until cheese is melted. Serve with your favorite burger condiments.

HINT: Don't ever squeeze patties with spatula. That will make them lose all their juicy goodness. And salt only after cooking meat; otherwise it will dry out the burgers.

2	**pounds ground turkey (⅓ dark meat)**
2	**tablespoons poultry seasoning**
2	**teaspoons black pepper**
	Salt
4	**slices Colby-Jack cheese**
4	**kaiser rolls**
	Assorted condiments

I Got Your Sandwich

My better half, Dot, owns the West Point Deli in West Point, Pennsylvania. Most of the truck drivers order sandwiches from her so they don't have to worry about making lunch on Fridays at the track. One week the truck driver for the No. 20 team forgot to place an order so I didn't have any goods for Tony Stewart and his boys. Tony sees me and flags me down. "Where's my Italian?" I let him know I didn't get an order. So he says, "I don't care if Scooter (the truck driver) places an order or not. Make sure you bring me an Italian every time you come to the track!" So I always bring a couple of 2 footers for him and Zippy (the crew chief).

Barbecue Beef Sandwiches
Serves 6

Make sure you have enough time before the race to make this recipe. It takes a little more than 3 hours, but it's worth it!

1 Place chuck roast in foil roasting pan, lightly sprinkle with pepper, and cover with aluminum foil. Preheat grill to 325°F. Place pan on lower cooking surface and bake with lid closed for 1 hour.

2 After 1 hour remove pan and cut roast into 4 to 6 smaller pieces. Add onion, garlic, salt (if desired), and splash some hot sauce (if desired) in the mix. Cover and put back on lower cooking surface to cook for 1 more hour.

3 At the end of the second hour remove pan and cut meat into smaller pieces. Stir to coat with the juices, cover, and put back on lower cooking surface to cook for 1 more hour.

4 After 3 hours total cooking time, remove pan and shred the meat. Add the barbecue sauce and mix thoroughly. Cover and place back on lower cooking surface. Split onion buns and place on upper cooking surface. Close lid and cook for another 8 to 12 minutes. Serve meat on toasted buns.

1	4-pound boneless chuck roast
	Black pepper
1	onion, diced
4	cloves garlic, crushed and diced
	Salt (optional)
	Louisiana hot sauce
1	18-ounce bottle Tony Stewart's "Smoke" Bar-B-Que sauce
6	large onion buns

Oh So Suite!

One of my personal sponsors is Pilgrim's Pride Chicken. They are based in Texas and have a suite at the Texas Motor Speedway. On one race weekend, my buddy Dan Emery, their vice president of marketing, invited me up to the suite to watch the Busch race. This was the first time I actually sat down and watched a race live other than from pit road since I started working in the garage in 1980. Let me tell you, this is the way to see a race. All the food and drink you can devour and instant replays on TV. No wonder everyone loves NASCAR! If you ever get the chance, spend the money and get into a suite. It's well worth it.

Yee Haw Coleslaw

Serves 6 to 8

There's nothing like some good ol' coleslaw as a side dish when you're eating barbecue.

1 Place the cabbage in a colander and add the bell pepper, celery, carrots, and radishes. Mix thoroughly. Sprinkle the 2 teaspoons salt over the cabbage mixture. Place colander over a slightly smaller bowl. The salt will help the mixture lose some of its water so it won't end up in the final mix.

2 To make the dressing, use a small stainless-steel mixing bowl. Stir together mayonnaise, vinegar, sugar, 1/4 teaspoon kosher salt, horseradish sauce (if desired), and white pepper. Whisk all the ingredients together. Cover and chill in the refrigerator or cooler for at least 1 hour.

3 Transfer cabbage mixture from the colander to a large salad bowl. Pour dressing into bowl and toss. Taste and adjust seasoning as desired.

HINT: For creamier coleslaw, add more mayonnaise.

1	head cabbage, shredded to make 8 to 10 cups
1	green bell pepper, seeded and finely diced
2/3	cup celery, finely diced
4	carrots, peeled and shredded
1/2	cup sliced radishes
2	teaspoons salt
1/2	cup mayonnaise
1	tablespoon white wine vinegar or lemon juice
1/2	teaspoon sugar
1/4	teaspoon kosher salt
1	tablespoon horseradish sauce (optional)
	Ground white pepper

Watch Your Gauge

Many new grills have a temperature gauge that can be removed and used as a meat thermometer. I think that's a pretty cool thing. Use the thermometer like drivers use their gauges to make sure everything is running at the right temperature. The thermometer is a must if you want to use your grill for baking. You can also use it to check the temperature of oil when you're deep frying. It's handy to check the doneness of meat, though hopefully after a while you should get a good "feel" for it. And if your grill doesn't come with a removable thermometer, I say go out and get one. It's worth the small price and great peace of mind.

Grilled & Thrilled Potatoes
Serves 6 to 12

Start this recipe first because it takes a while. Use russet potatoes because they can take the heat.

1 In a mixing bowl combine olive oil and the ¼ cup butter. Place potatoes in bowl and coat all sides with oil mixture

2 Preheat grill to medium high. Place potatoes faceup on upper cooking surface of grill and turn heat down to medium-low. Sprinkle with garlic salt, oregano, and pepper. Close lid and bake for 45 minutes to 1 hour or until tender. (Hint: Do not turn potatoes facedown or they will burn.)

3 Once the potatoes are done, remove and place on platter. Using a fork, mash the pulp of the potatoes while they are in the skin. Top with the ½ cup butter, sour cream, chives, and cheese, if desired.

½   cup extra-virgin olive oil
¼   cup butter, softened
6   large russet potatoes, cut in half lengthwise
1   tablespoon garlic salt
1   tablespoon dried oregano
1   tablespoon black pepper
½   cup butter, softened
16   ounces sour cream
1   bunch chives, finely chopped
    Shredded cheddar cheese, (optional)

We've Got a Winner!

After I started cooking for Goodyear, a friend asked me if going to the track had changed for me. I was kind of confused by the question, so I had to have him explain it. He said, "Well, since you're not working on a team, you can't win a race! How do you handle not being able to win?" I had to ponder on that one about a second before I replied, "Heck, I win every weekend! Last time I checked, every team uses Goodyear tires, and I work for them, so I win every race!"

Gas Man Baked Beans
Serves 6 to 8

As second gas man, I can tell you I've given gas to many famous drivers. Spread the love by giving some gas to your friends!

1 Place a large soup pot on the side burner. Combine the baked beans, pinto beans, kidney beans, brown sugar, maple syrup, barbecue sauce, and molasses. Bring up to temperature by starting the burner out on high with the lid on pot. Once up to temp, lower burner to medium. Stir often and cook for at least 1 hour, covered. Don't let the beans stick or burn!

2 Uncover pot and add salt, black pepper, and hot sauce to taste. Cook, uncovered, for 20 to 30 minutes to reduce liquid. Turn heat to low, cover, and cook for an additional 15 minutes. Turn off heat and let the pot coast.

HINT: This is a sweet recipe. If you prefer less sweetness, reduce the brown sugar, maple syrup, and molasses.

2	28-ounce cans baked beans (original style)
1	16-ounce can pinto beans, undrained
1	16-ounce can light red kidney beans, undrained
1/2	cup brown sugar, packed
1	cup maple syrup
1/2	cup barbecue sauce
1/4	cup molasses
	Salt
	Black pepper
	Louisiana hot sauce

Freezer Burn

As my sponsor, Pilgrim's Pride gives me all kinds of chicken products to cook. My favorite is boneless, skinless breasts. At one race I got behind on making lunch for the boys, so I started putting frozen chicken on the grill, much to the dismay of Dan, my buddy at Pilgrim's. After lunch was over, he commented on how good the chicken was, even though it started out frozen. I had to explain to him that if you sear both sides while they are frozen, the moisture stays inside while they finish roasting. About six months later I'm looking at a package of frozen breasts and there's a small note on the side: "No thawing required." Go figure!

Green Flag Salad with Raspberry Dressing
Serves 8 to 12

You can't beat the combo of flavors in this easy recipe!

1 The best bet is to make the vinaigrette at home and bring it in a shaker bottle with you. Process the raspberries in a food processor until berries are well broken up but not pureed. Pour berries into a mixing bowl. Add vinegar, salt, and pepper. Start mixing with a whisk, then slowly drizzle olive oil in while mixing. Blend well but don't overdo it. Pour it into a shaker and refrigerate.

2 Take the core out of the iceberg lettuce and shred lettuce. Shred the romaine and red leaf lettuce as well. Place in a large resealable salad bowl and add onion. Mix thoroughly and chill in cooler or refrigerator.

3 Serve in individual bowls when ready and add raspberry vinaigrette to taste.

1	pint fresh raspberries
¼	cup high-quality white wine vinegar
½	teaspoon salt
½	teaspoon white pepper
1	cup extra virgin olive oil
1	head iceberg lettuce
1	head romaine lettuce
1	head red leaf lettuce
1	Vidalia onion, halved and sliced thin

Hot Diggity Dog

When cooking dogs on the grill, roast them on the upper cooking surface—do not kill them on the lower surface. It should take more than 30 minutes before you see good caramelizing on the skin of the dogs and little strands of sweetness coming off them. Try to select a good beef dog; I usually get Ball Park Franks. Dale Earnhardt Sr. stopped by the grill one day at Michigan and asked if I was cooking Ball Parks. When I let him know I was, he grabbed a bun and dog and off he went. It was a shocker to me because he usually would never eat off of anybody's grill in the garage.

John's Mom's Apple Pie
Serves 6 to 8

My mother, Ethel, made this when I was a kid—it was quite the treat. She'd kill me if she knew I use premade piecrust.

1 On a bread board sprinkle flour generously. Roll out the piecrusts. Place a 9-inch pie pan facedown over one of the dough circles. Pick up pan and dough together and flip face side up. Pat and fit dough into pan. Trim excess dough off sides of the pan with a sharp knife.

2 In a mixing bowl stir together sugar and cinnamon. Add the apples and stir gently. Place the apple mixture in the dough-lined pan. Dot the top of the apple filling with pats of butter. Place second piece of dough over top of pie and work the edge into small ridges. Cut slits on top crust to vent.

3 Preheat grill to 425°F. Place pie on upper cooking surface. Close lid and bake for 50 to 60 minutes. Bake until crust is golden brown and apples are cooked through. Test doneness with a wire cake tester.

4 Serve warm or cold with a scoop of vanilla ice cream.

HINT: To keep the crust from browning too fast, wrap a 1-inch-wide strip of foil around the edge of the crust. Remove 15 minutes before the pie comes out of the grill.

Ingredients

Flour

- 1 15-ounce package rolled, refrigerated, unbaked piecrust
- 1 cup sugar
- 1 teaspoon cinnamon
- 2 McIntosh apples, cored, peeled, and sliced (2 cups)
- 4–5 Granny Smith green apples, cored, peeled, and sliced (5 cups)
- 1½ tablespoons butter
- ½ gallon vanilla ice cream

The South

Talladega & Atlanta

The South—red clay, red ants, rednecks, and of course there's catfish and crawfish, 100 percent humidity, peaches in bushels and on limbs, and the two fastest racetracks in the world—period!

The Talladega Superspeedway, located in Alabama, is just massive. It was built on the highest ground in the area, formerly used as an air base during the big one—World War II. Standing at the bottom of the banking in the turns watching a Cup car roar by roughly three stories above your head is a sensation that's hard to explain. I won't even try—you're on your own. Pit road alone is over a quarter-mile long! I'm glad they stop racing here in July because working in 100 degrees with 100 percent humidity would be against the law anywhere else.

"The Big One" is always a factor here. It's a wreck that winds up taking out up to half the field because everyone is bumper to bumper at about 190 mph. There have been many spectacular crashes on this track, including one that forced the mandating of restrictor plates. Bobby Allison took out more than a hundred yards of catch fence on the front stretch at well over 200 mph that unfortunately injured several fans with chunks of car parts along the way.

The party here is in the infield. The crowd gets going early and stays up all night. I've never been to Mardi Gras, but I'd have to say that after surviving Talladega you may feel like you could skip the Big Easy! Every type of motor home known to mankind will be found here. My personal favorites are the school buses turned party palaces painted black with the No. 3 for Dale Earnhardt Sr. on them! One year, I counted a dozen of them on race day.

Atlanta Motor Speedway was originally built as a true 1.5-mile oval with the turns at a half mile each. It was reconfigured in 1997 to resemble the layout at Charlotte with the exception that it is faster. Currently Atlanta has the fastest pole speed (197.478 mph set by Geoffrey Bodine) of all the tracks since NASCAR mandated restrictor plates at Talladega and Daytona. That'll blow your beer right out of your can-cozy.

One odd thing that these two tracks have in common is that they're both in states that observe blue laws prohibiting alcohol sales on Sundays. I'm no CPA, but these tracks must lose millions in beer sales on race day. One more thing, when driving from the city to the track near Hampton, don't count on finding your friends who told you to meet them at the Waffle House. I've had better luck with needles and haystacks.

On the Pole

When you think of the South you always think of a warm, sun-loving place. Atlanta can be a different kind of a deal. Back on the old schedule, we used to race there in November and March, and you could just as easily find yourself in freezing rain and snow. Anyway, Robby Gordon became our driver and in only the third race of the 1997 season, we were sitting on the pole. I couldn't believe it. This was one upstart that you definitely knew was for real. Robby just doesn't mess around when he's behind the wheel. But as we all know, starting from the pole is just that, a place to start. What counts in racing is where you finish.

Ragin' Cajun Creole Shrimp
Serves 4 to 6

You can't go to the South without having some killer shrimp. Serve this dish with dirty rice or straight up with Italian bread for dipping.

1 On side burner, heat ¼ cup of the butter in a skillet until melted. Add the onion, celery, red bell pepper, and garlic. Saute until tender. Remove and set aside.

2 Place a large saucepan on the burner and combine V8 juice, water, and hot sauce to taste. Bring to a boil, then add the sauteed vegetables. Simmer for 30 minutes. Add shrimp and cook for another 5 minutes or until shrimp turn pink.

3 Spread the remaining ¼ cup of the butter on the surface of the Italian bread and sprinkle with garlic salt to taste. Wrap in heavy foil. Preheat grill to medium-high and warm bread on upper cooking surface with lid closed for 5 to 10 minutes.

4 Pour shrimp mixture in large soup bowls and serve with garlic bread for dipping.

½	cup butter
1	onion, diced
3	stalks celery, sliced
1	red bell pepper, seeded and diced
2	cloves garlic, minced
2	16-ounce cans V8 juice
1	cup water
	Louisiana hot sauce
2–3	pounds large uncooked shrimp, cleaned, peeled, and deveined
1	loaf Italian bread, cut in half lengthwise
	Garlic salt

Talladega, Hooolieeee!

One weekend my buddy Eric and his friends got a motor home in the Talladega infield and I stayed with them Saturday night. We went for a stroll and I gotta tell you, you ain't seen nothin' until you spend Saturday night in the infield at Talladega! We walked by a school bus turned RV, and there's this guy sprawled in a lawn chair—he's obviously had a few too many. Then we ran into a cat standing in the bed of his pickup, dressed in Elvis baby blue Vegas garb with a karaoke machine and a light pointed up at himself. It was the worst Elvis you've ever heard, but the crowd loved it. It was like a big redneck Mardi Gras!

Catfish on a Hot Tin Roof
Serves 8

This one is good to make with hush puppies since you've already got the hot oil going!

1 Wash fillets and soak in a mixing bowl with enough water to cover fish, 2 tablespoons of the Tony's seasoning, and the paprika for 2 hours. Drain water without rinsing.

2 Mix cornmeal and the remaining 2 tablespoons Tony Chachere's seasoning together in a mixing bowl. Pour eggs into a second bowl and beat with a whisk. Place flour in a third mixing bowl. Dredge fillets in flour, then dip in eggs and coat with cornmeal mixture.

3 Preheat oil to 350°F. Drop fish in fryer and cook until golden brown, about 4 to 6 minutes. Remove and place on a plate lined with paper towels to drain. Serve with Shut Up Puppies (page 84) and Yee Haw Coleslaw (page 67).

Water
8   large catfish fillets, cut in half
4   tablespoons Tony Chachere's Original Creole seasoning
2   tablespoons paprika
2   cups yellow cornmeal
3   eggs
2   cups flour
Oil

Mudbugs

When the garage area was a little more fan-friendly and moving about wasn't a problem, my brother-in-law Terry Davis would come over to Talladega and put on one heck of a crawfish boil. We had to cook them out by our team owner Felix Sabates' motor coach. I have to admit, the cooler did raise a few noses, but c'mon, they're from the swamp! It took a while to cook all 125 pounds, but once they were done, no one was complaining about any odors anymore. Jimmy Makar from J.G.R. can really pack them away, let me tell you. Wally Dallenbach is no slouch either. He loves crawfish. I think the two of them must have eaten 75 pounds!

Serves 10 to 12

Straight from the Swamp Crawfish

The key to this recipe is to not let the crawfish crawl away before you cook 'em.

1 Clean crawfish by pouring into an ice chest full of water. Remove and dispose of dead crawfish. Drain cooler and add more water. Repeat 4 or 5 times until water runs clean.

2 Fill a large turkey fryer pot half full with water and bring to a slow boil. Add the dry crawfish boil and continue to boil for 15 minutes. Add potatoes, onions, and margarine; reduce heat to a simmer. When potatoes are almost tender, add the ears of corn. Cook 5 more minutes. Turn heat off and let stand 15 minutes. Remove vegetables and place in a foil roasting pan. Cover with aluminum foil.

3 Bring water to a rolling boil; add the lemons, the liquid boil, and hot sauce. Boil for 15 minutes. Add the crawfish and boil for another 5 minutes. Remove from heat and let stand until all the crawfish have sunk to the bottom. Drain and serve with the veggies.

1	sack live crawfish, about 35 to 40 pounds
1	ounce Zatarain's crawfish, shrimp & crab boil (dry)
5	pounds new potatoes, halved
5	large onions
2	cups margarine
18	ears frozen corn on the cob
10	lemons, cut in half
3	ounces Zatarain's shrimp & crab boil (liquid)
1	small bottle Louisiana hot sauce

Crew Chief?

One time I was set up to cook live on a TV show in Atlanta. The host came over and asked how to pronounce my last name, Youk. I told him and he repeated it back to me all wrong. So I said to remember it like this, "It's a rhyme—look, cook, book, Youk." He says he's got it. Then he asks how long I've been a crew chief. I tell him, "Not chief, CHEF." There's a big difference, especially to the drivers. He nods his head. The stage person goes, "OK, you're on in 5-4-3-2," and the host says, "I'm here with Big John Yowk, crew chief for Team Sabco." I hope any PR is good PR.

Shut Up Puppies

Serves 12

One race it was snowing. My brother-in-law, Terry, came up with this hotter-than-hot idea to warm things up a bit!

1 In a mixing bowl combine the cornmeal mix, flour, and seasoning. Stir in the eggs, corn, onion, and jalapeños. The batter will be thick. Some people like to add a dash of beer (if desired) for additional flavor.

2 Preheat oil in a deep fryer to 350°F. Dip an iced-tea spoon in a glass of water so the batter won't stick to the spoon. Then scoop batter into a round ball with the spoon and drop in fryer. Repeat with remaining batter. Fry until they turn over and are golden brown, about 2 to 3 minutes. Remove and place on a plate lined with paper towels to drain.

3 cups Aunt Jemima self-rising white cornmeal mix

½ cup self-rising flour

½ teaspoon Tony Chachere's Original Creole seasoning

2 eggs

1 16-ounce can cream-style corn

1 medium onion, finely diced

3 jalapeño peppers, seeded and finely diced (adjust heat up or down by using more or fewer jalapeños)

Beer (optional)

Oil

Wanna Ice Cream?

One year during a race it was boiling hot so me, Kyle and the whole crew decide to take a stroll down the front straightaway. We're just past turn 1 and looking through the fence when we see an ice cream stand. We're all dyin' because there's no way we can get to that stand. This couple sitting in the stands sees the drool coming out of our mouths and the wife comes over. "Hey, you guys want an ice cream?" That was all she had to say to get the guys worked up. A minute later she comes back with an ice cream for everyone and passes them through the fence. She wouldn't take our money. What a great fan!

Dirty, Rotten, Corrupt Rice
Serves 6 to 8

This recipe shows you how easy it is to make good food—and keep 'em coming back for more.

1 On the side burner saute the ground sausage in a large skillet, breaking it apart with a fork. Once cooked, add rice and stir. Add the chicken soup, mushroom soup, onion, bell pepper, celery, and water; mix thoroughly. Transfer mixture to a 9×13-inch foil roasting pan. Cover tightly with heavy duty aluminum foil.

2 Preheat grill to 325°F. Place pan on upper cooking surface and bake with grill lid closed for 1½ hours. Do not open foil cover until completely cooked.

HINT: For moister rice, add an extra ½ can of water.

1	pound ground hot Italian sausage
1½	cups uncooked rice
1	10¾-ounce can cream of chicken soup
2	10¾-ounce cans cream of mushroom soup
1	large onion, chopped
1	green bell pepper, seeded and chopped
3	stalks celery, diced
1	10¾-ounce soup can of water

What's for Lunch?

Let it be known that I love the outdoors and hunting. In 2000 I was able to hunt in five states: Pennsylvania, New Jersey, Connecticut, North Carolina, and Texas. I was able to bag a white-tailed buck in all of them, including a second in Jersey. Opening day in Connecticut was very good to me, and I got my buck, took it home, cut it up, and blasted off for Atlanta. I even stopped at Felix Sabates' place in North Carolina and fit in an afternoon muzzle-loader hunt. I wasn't due in Atlanta until Saturday, so when I got there early Friday morning I kind of took folks by surprise. But everyone knew that lunch would be a good thing!

Mama's Sweet Potato Casserole

Serves 8 to 12

I knew a lot of folks who didn't like sweet potatoes. This recipe changed them into total fans—honest!

1 On the side burner boil the sweet potatoes in a large pot of water until tender. Drain after cooking and mash the potatoes. Stir in granulated sugar, ½ cup of the butter, eggs, vanilla, and milk. Spread the mixture into a greased 9×13-inch foil roasting pan.

2 For the topping melt the remaining ⅓ cup butter in a saucepan. Remove from heat and add brown sugar, flour, pecans, and coconut, (if desired). Spread this mixture over the top of the sweet potatoes.

3 Preheat the grill to 350°F. Place foil pan on upper cooking surface and bake for 25 to 30 minutes with the lid closed. Serve with a dollop of sour cream or whipped cream, (if desired).

- 3 cups peeled and quartered sweet potatoes (about 4 large)
- ¾ cup granulated sugar
- 1⅓ cups butter, divided
- 2 eggs, beaten
- 1 teaspoon vanilla extract
- ⅓ cup milk
- ½ cup brown sugar, packed
- ⅓ cup flour
- 1 cup pecans, chopped
- 1 cup coconut (optional)
- 8 ounces sour cream (optional)
- 8 ounces whipped cream (optional)

Texas Sweets

There's a restaurant in Anniston, Alabama called Top of the River our team always tried to go to. We'd get a big table and order the catfish and hush puppies. As a palate cleanser, they have pickled onions on the table. One time, Tony Glover, the crew chief, says, "I wonder what kind of onions these are?" I say, "I'm guessing Oso or Texas Sweets." Glover goes, "Nah, Vidalia." To shut us up, our tire guy asks the waitress to find out. She comes back and says, "You can't have the recipe." I say, "We don't want the recipe, just the type of onion." She comes back with "Texas Sweets." I say to Glover, "You stick to wrenchin' the car, and I'll stick to the cooking!"

Fry, Fry Again Green Tomatoes

Serves 6

If you see big green tomatoes, buy 'em and try this recipe. They'll make your infield friends green with envy.

1 Cut the tomatoes into ¼-inch slices, discarding the ends. Place flour, eggs, and bread crumbs in three separate bowls. Prepare the tomatoes by first dredging in the flour and shaking off the excess. Next dip in egg wash and then coat with bread crumbs.

2 Heat oil in large skillet on side burner to 350°F on medium-high. Fry tomatoes until golden brown on both sides, about 4 to 5 minutes. Place on a paper towel-lined plate to drain excess oil.

3 Serve straight up or with ketchup, if desired. I like a light smear of mayonnaise on mine.

12 green tomatoes (baseball size)

2 cups flour

4 eggs, beaten

4 cups Italian-style bread crumbs

3 cups vegetable oil
   Ketchup (optional)
   Mayonnaise (optional)

He's Bored

I like Robby Gordon. He's won races in every type of car he's been in—from trophy trucks and Indy cars to my favorite, stock cars. The first time he drove at Talladega for us was the year he left the Indy car series. While cruising around the track midpack at 200 mph in the first practice session, our crew chief asked him how he liked the speed. His reply seemed cocky at the time: "I'm bored." Looking back I can see why. He was used to doing 230 mph on the straightaway at Indianapolis!

You're Not a Fried Turkey
Serves 8 to 10

This takes some time to prepare. Remember to thaw your turkey in the fridge for 4 days before starting the prep on this recipe!

1 Prepare the turkey the day before by washing it completely inside and out. Pat the turkey dry. Mix the salt, pepper, seasoning, and garlic powder together. Use ⅔ of this mixture to rub all over the turkey.

2 To make the injection sauce, melt butter and mix in the remaining seasoning mixture from step 1. Add the hot sauce and blend. Inject the mixture all over the bird. Place the turkey back in refrigerator.

3 Place a large pot on a turkey fryer and fill halfway with peanut oil. Heat oil to 360°F. Submerge turkey slowly into oil. (Wear gloves and a long-sleeve shirt to protect yourself.) When turkey is totally submerged, start timing. As turkey cooks, reduce heat and maintain 325°F. Fry for 3½ minutes per pound. The turkey is done when golden brown and floating. The internal temperature should be 165°F. Remove and let turkey rest 20 minutes before carving.

1	12- to 14-pound turkey
¼	cup seasoned salt
¼	cup black pepper
½	cup Tony Chachere's Original Creole seasoning
¼	cup garlic powder
1	cup butter
¼	cup Louisiana hot sauce
2-3	gallons peanut oil

Papa's Pecan Pie
Serves 8

Nothing beats a slice of pecan pie for dessert. Top it off with some good vanilla ice cream.

1 In a mixing bowl beat together the eggs, sugar, salt, butter, and syrup. Once mixture is blended, stir in the pecans. Place the piecrust in a 9-inch pie pan; pour mixture into the piecrust.

2 Preheat grill to 375°F. Place pie on upper cooking surface. Close lid and bake for 40 to 50 minutes. Remove and let cool.

3 Serve cold or slightly warm with a big scoop of vanilla ice cream.

HINT: To keep the crust from browning too fast, wrap a 1-inch-wide strip of foil around the edge of the crust. Remove 15 minutes before the pie comes out of the grill.

3	eggs
2/3	cup sugar
1/3	teaspoon salt
1/3	cup butter, melted
1	cup dark Karo corn syrup
1	cup pecans, halved
1	premade piecrust
1/2	gallon vanilla ice cream

The Carolinas

Charlotte & Darlington

The Carolinas, North and South, mean tobacco, moonshine, paved cow trails called roads, the roots of stock car racing, and two legendary giants—Charlotte and Darlington.

Charlotte came about in the 1960s and is celebrated as the home of NASCAR racing. Charlotte's 1.5-mile oval has been copied by both Atlanta and Texas and hosts the longest race on the circuit—600 miles. The racing here is usually side by side, producing some wild finishes and spectacular last-lap crashes. They really let it all hang out in the All-Star race. This is your basic "dash for cash" where you don't score points for the season and you don't hold on to friendships for long. Go on—take the money and run.

I'd recommend taking a day to tour the race shops. Just about all of the teams are based in Mooresville and Concord. Most shops have a viewing area and gift store. While you're in Mooresville, there are a couple of race-themed restaurants to check out. Lancaster's Barbecue has a *Days of Thunder* theme going on, and Big Daddy's is known for its oysters and seafood; just look for the race cars on the roof! If you've flown into town for the race and haven't had an opportunity to eat until you're waiting for your flight out, the Stock Car Cafe in the airport is your last chance for catching a race-themed meal.

For those of you who are looking for the real racing experience, sign up and learn how to drive a stock car at the Richard Petty Driving Experience at the track. It's a lot more fun than the spinning teacups at Disneyland. I ought to know, I've done it myself.

Darlington Raceway is the original superspeedway, "The Lady in Black." She was built in 1950, long before the stock car craze took hold. It's a track that drivers either love or hate. There's no middle ground here. Kyle Petty was being interviewed at a Darlington race and suggested they should just fill the whole darn thing up with water and turn it into a bass fishing lake! Now and then, you'll find quite a few drivers who agree. The track has an odd shape due to the landowner's demand that his minnow pond not be disturbed. The egg shape has made crew chiefs scratch their heads ever since, trying to figure out a setup for this place. Then there is the famous "Darlington Stripe," the scrape most drivers put on their car after hitting the wall coming out of turns 2 and 4! Heck, I've even got one on my old pickup truck!

Since Darlington is so close to Charlotte, most of the teams travel home each day, which meant I didn't stay in town all that often. You'll just have to check with your hotel's concierge for the best local restaurants.

The Snowman 300

Back in the day, we used to leave speed weeks in Daytona and go right to Richmond. It was still winter in Richmond in February, and the weather wasn't always looking out for your best interests. I can remember getting to the hotel, and the snow was piling up. As far as we knew, there was still going to be an event at the track over the weekend. It turned out to be the snowman sculpture 300—no race, but tons of snow. Now, what with Phoenix, Vegas, and California on board, those snow days are no more. I kinda miss 'em, and then again, I kinda don't.

Colder Than Snot Chili
Serves 12

I used to make this in Rockingham when we would go there after Daytona. This stuff will warm you up on a cold spring day.

1 In a large pot on the side burner, place olive oil and butter, and heat to medium-high. Add onions and cook until translucent, about 5 minutes.

2 Add ground beef to onions and brown. Reduce heat to medium.

3 Add green and red bell peppers, tomatoes, and chili sauce. Add 1 can each of the *undrained* beans (if desired, add more beans to your personal taste). Stir thoroughly and bring to boil. Add the chili powder and black pepper (if desired, add more to your personal taste). Turn heat down to medium-low; cover and simmer for at least 1 hour.

4 Serve in bowls and top with cheese. Dig in with Frito scoops—a great way to eat this chili!

3	tablespoons olive oil
1/8	cup butter
2	onions, coarsely chopped
2	pounds 90% lean ground beef
2	green bell peppers, seeded and coarsely chopped
2	red bell peppers, seeded and coarsely chopped
2	tomatoes, coarsely chopped
1	16-ounce can crushed tomatoes
1	12-ounce jar chili sauce
2	16-ounce cans dark red kidney beans
2	16-ounce cans red kidney beans
2	16-ounce cans pinto beans
1	28-ounce can pork & beans
4	ounces chili powder
4	tablespoons black pepper
16	ounces shredded cheddar and Monterey Jack cheese blend
1	2-pound bag Fritos scoops

Funeral for a Fowl

One thing I can't stress enough is to pay attention to your grill when you've got food cooking on it. A distraction can lead to disaster or worse—inedible food! When we were preparing the chicken for this photo, our food prep superstar, Mike, was yakkin' on a cell phone, and the next thing we know the grill is blazing like the Chicago Fire, only we didn't have Mrs. O'Leary's cow on it. I honestly didn't know you could get the internal temperature of a gas grill past 800°! Hey, even the best can have a bad day grilling!

Banjo Pickin' Rubbed Chicken

Serves 4

Salt dries some of the fat and makes the skin crisp when you grill. But wash your hands before you get those banjos dueling!

1 Wash the chickens inside and out. Dry off and salt the skin. Mix the herb chicken and poultry seasonings together and rub all over chickens; sprinkle some on the inside as well.

2 Rinse out the inside of two 16-ounce iced-tea cans. In a saucepan on the side burner, dissolve the bouillon cubes in the water over medium-heat. Pour equal amounts of chicken broth into each iced-tea can but do not fill all the way.

3 Preheat grill to 325°F to 350°F. Place the iced-tea cans on the lower cooking surface and put chickens over the cans, legs down. Close lid and cook for about 1 hour. Make sure the temperature of the grill stays between 325°F and 350°F. The chickens are done when the internal temperature is 160°F.

HINT: Make sure the grill is level and the chickens are stable.

2	whole frying chickens
2	tablespoons salt
½	cup McCormick herb chicken seasoning
2	tablespoons poultry seasoning
2	chicken bouillon cubes
4	cups water

A Meal Fit for The King

One night before qualifying at Charlotte, I cooked a huge boneless beef rib roast with baked spuds and veggies for the boys. When someone was ready to eat, I'd slice off a piece, drag it over the heat on the lower surface, and load up the plate with all the goods. "The King," Richard Petty, walks by and points to the end of the prime rib and says, "I think that's my piece right there." Well, you can't deny The King a meal, so I loaded up a plate for him and off he went! I got a ton of compliments about dinner that night.

Sit Down Standing Ribeye

Serves 10 to 12

I like making this for the guys on qualifying night at Charlotte.

1 Rub olive oil all over the surface of the roast. Sprinkle seasoning over roast as well.

2 Preheat grill to high. Place roast on lower cooking surface and sear all sides of the meat. Once the meat is seared, reduce heat to medium and cook the meat in the center of the grill, fat side up, with lid closed. Cook for another 20 to 30 minutes. A meat thermometer is a must at this point: 140°F to 145°F for rare; 150°F to 155°F for medium; and at 170°F send it to the trash! I like mine slightly rare.

3 To finish it off, slice roast into ⅜- to ½-inch-thick slices and drag each side over the bottom cooking surface before serving; this should take less than a minute or it will be overcooked. Serve with A.1. steak sauce, if desired.

¼ cup olive oil

1 6- to 8-pound boneless beef rib roast

¼ cup McCormick Montreal steak seasoning

1 bottle A.1. steak sauce (optional)

I Can Drive That

One Christmas, Kyle Petty gave the whole crew 30 laps at the Richard Petty Driving Experience in Charlotte as a gift. Talk about a fun time! You really get a taste of what it's like to drive those cars we work on all the time. Doing over 150 mph on the backstretch was quite the thrill. And making the left turn going into turn 3 was scary! It really gave me some new perspective on the drivers who make it look so easy. I think I'll stick to cooking. You might lose an eyebrow now and then, but man, it's a lot safer!

Hot on Their Tail Beef Sandwiches

Serves 6

This is a great dish to preassemble at home and bring with you to the track. I like serving this dish on cold days.

1 Place half of the lunch meat in a 10×13×3-inch foil pan. Pour one jar of the brown gravy over the meat and cover with half of the onion. Layer the rest of the lunch meat over the onion and pour the second jar of gravy over the meat; cover with the rest of the onion. Pour water over the meat mixture. Cover with plastic wrap and then foil for transporting. Before heating, remove the foil and release the plastic from the edges of the pan. Lay plastic directly over the meat. Put foil back on top of the pan and seal.

2 Preheat grill to medium-high. Place pan on lower cooking surface and close lid. When the top of the pan starts to feel warm, reduce the heat to medium or medium-low. Total heating time is 30 to 35 minutes. Meanwhile, place split rolls facedown on upper cooking surface for the last 5 minutes to toast. Discard foil and plastic wrap after the meat is heated through.

3 Fill toasted rolls with meat mixture and serve with horseradish sauce. Season with salt and pepper to taste.

3 pounds precooked roast beef lunch meat, sliced

2 8-ounce jars Heinz brown gravy

½ onion, thinly sliced

½ cup water

6 kaiser rolls, split

Horseradish sauce

Salt

Black pepper

Pee Dee's

One reason I love going to the spring race at Darlington is the Pee Dee's state farmers' market. Nothing is growing yet back home, so I have a chance to get one up on the neighbors. If you saw my yard, you'd know what I mean. The market is about 15 minutes away from the track, so I'll make time to stop by and pick up some fresh produce, but more important, I always get my spring flowers from there. I'll get them back to the house outside of Philly and put them in the flower beds. The neighbors always ask, "Where did you get the flowers?" And I always reply, "The farmer's market," as if they have any chance of finding it!

Single-Wide Green Beans

Serves 4

Let's do a real simple recipe here. It's crazy that it's so easy, and you're not gonna believe how tasty it is!

1 Cut tips off beans and cut in half (if desired). Place a steamer on the side burner and combine water and salt in pot. Place green beans and onion in the top of the steamer and bring water to a boil. Reduce heat and simmer, covered. Check the doneness by tasting; the beans should be tender but still have a little crunch.

2 Remove beans and onion and place in serving platter. Toss with butter and vegetable seasoning.

1   pound whole green beans

1   quart water

1   tablespoon salt

1   large yellow onion, cut into wedges

¼   cup butter, softened

1   tablespoon Prudhomme's Vegetable Magic

Goin' on Green

I was spotting for Kevin Lepage at the Busch race in Charlotte. The spotters usually stand on the roof of the suites on the front stretch, but I got to do it from Felix Sabates' domed condo in turn 1. He was having quite the shindig with all the partygoers dressed to the nines. I'm gobbling up all the catered food when we get a caution flag, so I figure I'd better hit the little chef's room while I have a chance! I get to the bathroom and the door's locked! I wait and wait and wait and right before the door pops open, the crew chief yells, "Green, green, green!" I tell you, that was the fastest bathroom break in history, 13 seconds flat!

Double-Wide Baked Potatoes
Serves 8

This recipe is for the motor home race fan who has electricity. Just imagine if they made double-wides. You'd need a huge infield!

1 Using a fork, poke holes all over the potato skins. Cook on high in the microwave for 10 to 12 minutes or until fork-tender. Wrap each potato individually in heavy-duty foil. Finish cooking on grill with lid closed on medium heat for 60 to 90 minutes.

2 While potatoes bake, cook bacon in a skillet on the side burner. Make sure to cook until bacon is crisp. Place on a plate lined with paper towels to drain and cool. Once cool, crumble and place in bowl.

3 Remove potatoes from grill and serve with bacon, butter, sour cream, chives, and cheese, if desired.

8	large russet baking potatoes, washed and scrubbed
8	slices bacon
1/2	cup butter, softened
8	ounces sour cream
4	chives, finely chopped
	Shredded cheddar cheese (optional)

My Darlington Stripe

One year, we blew up early in the race at Darlington. I know how bad traffic gets leaving the track, so I'm rushing to get out of the infield ahead of the mobs. I help the guys load the hauler, then I load up all my cooking stuff in my truck and speed off. As I go through the tunnel (which is now under turn 1), I hear this horrible scraping noise! I look over and my passenger-side mirror is folded in and has this big white scrape on it. After going to "The Lady in Black" for years, I unintentionally got my first Darlington stripe. I just wish the insurance had covered it.

Who Drove Off with My House Salad? Serves 8 to 10

This salad is so simple and tasty, and you can make it anywhere.

1 Mix lettuces, cucumbers, onion, carrots, red and green bell peppers, celery, and radishes (if desired) into a large stainless-steel bowl. Cover and keep chilled until ready to serve. Keep the tomatoes chilled in a separate covered container.

2 Combine the balsamic vinegar and the rice wine vinegar in a small bowl. Drizzle the olive oil in slowly and whisk together, making an emulsion.

3 Just before serving, place tomatoes in the salad and drizzle with dressing. Gently toss everything together and season with salt and white pepper.

1	head iceberg lettuce, cored and chopped
1	head romaine lettuce, cored and chopped
1	head red leaf lettuce, cored and chopped
2	cucumbers, striped and sliced into coins
1	sweet onion, chopped
2–3	carrots, peeled, cut into sticks
1	red bell pepper, diced
1	green bell pepper, seeded and diced
2–3	celery stalks, chopped
1	small bag radishes, cut into coins (optional)
2–3	tomatoes, cut into wedges
$^1/_4$–$^1/_2$	cup balsamic vinegar
2	tablespoons rice wine vinegar
1	cup olive oil
	Salt
	White pepper

Hot Spots

By all means, get to know your grill, especially where the hot and not-so-hot areas are. Always start off the cooking process on a high heat, then reduce the heat to maintain the oven temperature while the lid is closed. It is too tempting to cook on high heat all the time so you can get stuff done in a hurry. Do that and you're gonna get shown the black flag! Rotate the food from hot spots to not-so-hot spots. This makes for even cooking and getting things done at the same time.

Bad-Breath Garlic Bread

Serves 6 to 8

After eating this garlic bread, don't plan on picking up any hotties or stud muffins at the track unless you feed 'em too!

1 Cut bread in half lengthwise. Spread equal amounts of butter on each half. Sprinkle equal amounts of minced garlic, garlic powder, and garlic salt on each half. Put the bread halves back together and wrap in heavy-duty foil.

2 Preheat grill to 350°F. Place bread on upper cooking surface and close the lid. (If you don't have an upper cooking surface, place a baking pan underneath the bread to prevent burning.) Bake for 10 minutes.

1	loaf Italian bread
¼	cup butter, softened
6–8	cloves garlic, minced
2	pinches garlic powder
2	pinches garlic salt

Need a Paint Job?

Jim Sutton, one of our team's head fabricators, was involved in a fender bender and had to replace the rear quarter panel on his truck. It was still in primer when some of the guys in the paint shop painted "Super Yankee" on the side. They thought it was funny since Jim was a northern boy—from Chicago. When I was down for the race at Charlotte he asked me to paint the thing, so I drove it back to Pennsylvania and went to work on it. Some folks don't realize it, but I won some serious awards for body painting in my day. I had it done before the next race at Dover. It's always good to help out a fellow Yankee.

Not Commie
Red Beans & Rice

Serves 12 to 16

Sometimes I come up with a recipe on the fly. Sterling Marlin was bugging me to make this stuff, so I gave it a shot!

1 Combine water and white rice in a saucepan on the side burner. Bring to a boil. Cover and reduce heat to a simmer for 20 minutes or until liquid is absorbed. Remove from heat.

2 In another large pan on the side burner cook both boxes of red beans and rice according to package directions but do not use the seasoning packets at this time.

3 Preheat grill to medium high. In a medium foil pan, combine butter, garlic, and onions. Add *salt*, *black pepper*, and *crushed red pepper flakes* to taste. Put pan on upper cooking surface and saute onion mixture 5 minutes. Add shrimp to pan.

4 Season chicken with chicken seasoning and steak with steak seasoning. Place chicken and steak on lower cooking surface and cook with lid closed until chicken is almost done (150°F) and steak is medium-rare (145°F). Remove from heat and cut into ½-inch cubes.

5 When the boxed red beans and rice is done, add meat, white rice, canned beans, and 1 of the seasoning packets. Simmer, covered, on medium low for 30 to 45 minutes.

2	cups water
1	cup uncooked white rice (not instant)
2	boxes Zatarain's red beans and rice
¼	cup butter
4	cloves garlic, minced
1	onion, finely diced
1½	pounds large shrimp, peeled and deveined
4	boneless, skinless chicken breast halves
	McCormick Montreal chicken seasoning
2	12-ounce boneless New York strip steaks
	McCormick Montreal steak seasoning
1	23-ounce can dark red kidney beans, undrained
2	16-ounce cans pinto beans, undrained

Driving Practice

When I was working for Team Sabco, I got a notice that the pit crew was needed at the shop for practice. So I hop in the truck and make the 8-hour drive down to Charlotte. When I met Jim Sutton at the gate to get in, he was wondering why I was there. I show him the memorandum and he starts to laugh. He lets me know that the gas men are never needed for the practices. I guess I got some driving practice in that day—like I needed it!

You Have to Be Bananas John

Serves 4

This dessert has a nice kick to it. Make sure you're of legal drinking age when making this since it has peach brandy in it!

1 Place a large frying pan on the side burner of your grill and heat to medium. Melt the butter and then stir in the brown sugar. Allow mixture to simmer 5 minutes to caramelize the sugar. Add bananas and cook on both sides until golden brown. Remove from heat. Add peach brandy to the pan. Light the brandy with a camping lighter and let the flame burn out on its own. This means the residual alcohol has burned off.

2 Arrange four banana pieces in a spoke pattern on a plate and dust with powdered sugar. Place a scoop of ice cream in the center of the plate. Drizzle with some of the syrup in the pan.

¼   cup butter
¼   cup brown sugar, packed
4   bananas, peeled and quartered
½   cup peach brandy
    Powdered sugar
1   quart French vanilla ice cream

The Northeast

Loudon & Watkins Glen

This has to be some of the prettiest country the NASCAR circuit offers. Lush hills, valleys, agriculture, horses, Finger Lakes, home of the Erie Canal, and White Mountains' majesty. It's easy to see why the early settlers decided to set up towns around here, though after the first winter I'd be looking for some swampland in Florida. Still it sure is a nice place to visit a couple of racetracks.

There's just something about wine country and road racing. The track at Watkins Glen in New York rises about 10 stories (105 vertical feet) from the bottom of the "Esses" to the top of the back straightaway … it'll pop your ears. The track is the second road course on the circuit with its famous turn out on the backstretch. This is a thing called "the inner loop," and it's there to slow the cars down so they don't all become pancakes on the wall. The Glen is also known to be the home of the "ringers," drivers who specialize in road courses only, including some big names from Canada. *Parlez-vous* "in the wall"?

There's tons to do in the Northeast. The fresh produce stands along all the roadsides in the Finger Lakes district make it easy and cheap to get good sweet corn. You'll enjoy it with a nice sweet wine, available at every winery.

Going to a race should include a side trip or two. From The Glen you can make it to Niagara Falls within two hours. Bring your own barrel.

Loudon is a flat, one-mile oval known for its tight corners and was the first superspeedway to be built after man landed on the moon. Turn 3 of "The Magic Mile" was literally carved out of a hillside. They scooped out 30,000 cubic yards of rock ledge to give the fans more space.

Of course, fresh seafood is one of my favorites when I'm up in Loudon. Portland, Maine, is due east about an hour away from the track, and there are a ton of seafood restaurants to choose from. You can also get fresh seafood to go from the Harbor Fish Market. The place smells like the ocean, which is a good sign, 'cause if it smells like fish then it can't be too fresh!

Loudon is also near Concord, the capital of New Hampshire. Most of the teams stay there on race weekends. The old historic downtown has a number of really good restaurants and pubs to check out. One thing you've got to do while in New Hampshire is pick up a year's supply of maple syrup—this is where it comes from. Did you know that it takes 40 gallons of sweet crude maple tree sap to make 1 gallon of premium syrup? That stuff is liquid gold.

No Wining

What a coincidence. The other road course on the circuit, The Glen, is in wine country too! It's totally different from Sonoma, but I think it's every bit as good. The scenery in the Finger Lakes region is phenomenal. And if you drive around Seneca Lake north of the track, you can hit around two dozen wineries. The wine in New York tends to be sweeter than your traditional West Coast varietals. The Rieslings and ice wines are the standouts. When you get to Geneva on the north end of the lake, grab lunch at my buddy George's bar, The Inland Reef. It's a great local pub on the west side of town.

Upper Crusted Salmon
Serves 4

The crust on this salmon is amazing. Just be sure not to overcook the salmon once it's on the grill.

1 Cut fillet into 4 half-pound pieces and remove the pin bones. To do this, just rub your palm over the fillet and stop when you feel a bone. Pull it out with a little pair of pliers (nice and clean, of course). Mix salt, pepper, and dillweed together. Rub about 1 tablespoon of the softened butter generously over both sides of the fillets. Set remaining butter aside. Season fillets on both sides with the dry seasoning mix.

2 On a large plate mix macadamia nuts, pecans, and walnuts together. Coat both sides of each fillet with the nut mixture. On the side burner heat a large baking skillet to 350°F. (A baking skillet has a metal handle with no plastic.) Pour in oil and remaining butter. Place fillets skin sides down in pan and cook for 3 to 4 minutes. Flip over and cook on flesh side for 2 minutes.

3 Preheat grill to 400°F. Turn fish back over in pan and drain most of the oil, leaving about 3 tablespoons in the pan. Place on lower cooking surface and close lid. Bake for an additional 7 to 10 minutes or until salmon flakes easily with a fork.

1	2-pound salmon fillet (or two 1-pound fillets)
2	tablespoons butter, softened
2	teaspoons salt
1	teaspoon black pepper
1	teaspoon dried dillweed
½	cup butter, softened
¼	cup macadamia nuts, finely chopped
¼	cup pecans, finely chopped
¼	cup walnuts, finely chopped
1	cup extra-virgin olive oil

Lobsta

One of the benefits of traveling is all the different people I get to meet. In Loudon one year, I made the mistake of paying retail for lobster. Cost a fortune! At the following spring race I met Meredith Manning, the morning show host on Q-97 in Portland, Maine. I took her and a friend on the nickel tour of the joint and asked them to join the boys at Goodyear for lunch. They loved the food, but Meredith thought we needed lobster. I told her it cost about as much as a car, and sure enough, she said she had connections. Now at every fall race, she hooks me up with the goods! Nothing beats good friends and good lobster (at a great price).

Oh Say Can You Sea Lobsta & Steamas *Serves 6*

My friend, Meredith, hosts a radio show in Maine. She hooked me up with the best lobster guy around. Man, do I owe her!

1 Pour 2 to 2½ gallons of water in a turkey fryer. Bring water to a rolling boil. Plunge the lobsters in the pot headfirst. Toss in a good handful of seaweed. (The fish packer should have packed the lobsters in seaweed and ice.) Boil for 10 to 12 minutes after lobsters turn red. Remove lobsters and place in a clean cooler or covered foil roasting pan to keep warm while cooking clams.

2 Dump lobster water out and refill turkey fryer with 1½ gallons of water. Bring water to a rolling boil again. Place clams in basket and lower into boiling water. Clams are done when the shells open (approximately ⅛ inch to ¼ inch), not when they start screaming, "We're done here, let us out!" Remove and place in a foil roasting pan.

3 On the side burner, melt the butter in a saucepan and add garlic. Season lobster and clams with salt and pepper to taste. Serve with melted butter for dipping.

4	gallons water
6	lobsters (approximately 1¼ pounds each)
12	dozen clams, scrubbed
1	cup butter
4	cloves garlic, minced
	Salt
	Black pepper

Just Testing

One year at a test session at The Glen, the track workers let us take our rent-a-cars out to see what we could do. They ran the timing and scoring so we could see who was fastest. There were several teams at the session, and some of the Cup drivers got into the mix. Of course, I had to show everyone how it was done. When I pulled back into the pits, one of the track workers starts to give me an earful. "What the heck are you doing?" he asks me. "You ran faster than Dale (Earnhardt Sr.) did in his rent-a-car!" I wasn't sure if I really believed him, but later that same day, Sr. walked by, punched me in the arm, and walked off without saying a word.

In the Pot-Hole Chicken
Serves 4

Start after breakfast and forget about it. Fans with motor homes, use a slow cooker. Tailgaters, use the grill and a roasting pot.

1 Wash chicken completely, inside and out. Pat dry with a paper towel. Rub breast side of chicken with ¼ cup of the butter. Combine the 2 tablespoons salt, 1 tablespoon pepper, poultry seasoning, and paprika. Sprinkle bird with the salt mixture, inside and out.

2 For a slow cooker: Combine water and remaining ¼ cup butter in the bottom of pot. Place the chicken breast side up in the pot and cover. Turn slow cooker to high and cook for 1 hour. After 1 hour flip the breast side down and reduce heat to low. Cook for an additional 5 to 6 hours.

3 For grill cooking: Use the same cooking instructions as above, except put the ingredients in a covered roasting pot. Place pot on lower cooking surface of the grill and heat to medium-high (350°F). Close lid and cook for 1 hour. After 1 hour flip chicken and reduce heat to just above low. Cook for an additional 5 to 6 hours.

4 Turn side burner on high; pour 2 cups of salted water into steamer. Place onion, broccoli, and cauliflower into steamer basket and let 'er cook until veggies are crisp-tender, about 10 minutes. Pull 'em out, butter 'em up with the 2 tablespoons butter, and dig in. Season with salt and pepper.

1	whole fryer chicken
½	cup butter
2	tablespoons salt
1	tablespoon black pepper
1	tablespoon poultry seasoning
2	teaspoons paprika
½	cup water
1	Vidalia onion, chopped
1	head broccoli, cut into florets
1	head cauliflower, cut into florets
2	tablespoons butter
	Salt
	Black pepper

Oh Deer!

I'm an avid deer hunter. Some might even say I'm a little crazy about it. But if you happen to be one too, you need to stop by the Ranch 226 bar on Highway 226 west of The Glen. They have the most amazing display of mounted deer. There are a couple of walls with about 40 trophy mounts on them. I'm not sure if someone donated them or if the bartender got them, but it's probably a good conversation starter. Their happy hour is pretty good, if I remember right.

Bambi Burgers
Serves 8

I like to cook these, minus the antlers. If the deer was picked up as roadkill, minus the grille fragments and antifreeze!

1 Wet your hands with water or coat with butter to prevent venison from sticking to them while making the patties. Make eight ½-pound patties. Wrap each individually in plastic wrap and freeze.

2 Preheat grill to medium high. Dress frozen burgers with olive oil, steak seasoning, and garlic powder. Place burgers on lower cooking surface and close lid. Cook burgers to medium (150°F). Don't overcook because the meat is so lean. Toast buns on upper cooking surface.

3 Serve with your favorite burger condiments.

HINT: The doneness of venison is tough to judge if you base it on color. Venison is much deeper red than beef and will look uncooked when it is medium and if it's pink, it's past well done. This is a great time to use your meat thermometer so that you don't overcook your venison burger.

4	pounds ground venison
1	cup olive oil
¼	cup Dale's steak seasoning
2	tablespoons garlic powder
8	hamburger buns, split
	Assorted condiments

Jeff Who?

I was driving Kyle Petty out of the track at The Glen after qualifying one Friday when all of a sudden he yells, "Turn this thing around." I got the car turned around and Kyle directs me through some parked cars to a group of race fans. He gets out and walks over to a lady in a wheelchair wearing a Kyle Petty hat. She was shocked beyond belief. How he spotted her in the crowd, I will never know. Anyway, he spends some time with her and her friends talking and signing autographs. One of her friends is wearing some Jeff Gordon apparel and takes it off and throws it in the trash. He says to Kyle, "I'm your No. 1 fan for life now!"

Shut Your Clam Chowder
Serves 8 to 10

I ordered 600 steamers once in New Hampshire and ended up with 5,000 of the things. This soup helped finish them off.

1 Pour 1½ gallons of water in a turkey fryer. Bring water to a boil and place the clams in the cooking basket; gently lower into water. Cook until the clams open, about 5 to 7 minutes; remove from boiling water immediately. Remove the clams from the shells and discard the beard covering. Set clams aside to cool. Pour the cooking water through a fine-mesh strainer into a clean bowl for later use.

2 On the side burner place a large soup pot and set heat to medium-high. Saute onion in 1 tablespoon of the butter. Add the potatoes and saute 3 to 5 minutes. Add half-and-half, cream, and remaining butter. Ladle all but 1 cup of clam broth into the pot, making sure not to pick up any grit from the bottom of the bowl. Set aside the 1 cup of clam broth. Reduce heat to a simmer and cover. Stir the soup often.

3 Place corn in soup. Chop up half of the clams and leave the other half whole. Add clams to the mixture. Keep stirring. If you think the soup is too runny, you can thicken it by adding the ¼ cup flour to the 1 cup reserved clam broth and mix thoroughly; add to simmering soup. Total cooking time is 45 to 60 minutes. Season to taste with salt and pepper.

1½ gallons water

12 dozen clams, scrubbed

1 large onion, diced

2 cups butter, divided

6 cups peeled and diced potatoes (½-inch dice)

2 quarts half-and-half

1 pint heavy cream

3 ears fresh sweet corn, cleaned and cut off cob

¼ cup flour (optional for thickening)

Salt

Black pepper

The Hunting Camp

I got introduced to "The Bear," John Venuti, years ago by one of the crew guys on our team. I started going to his annual party on the Watkins Glen race weekend at his hunting camp. After a few years, I offered to cook and have been doing so ever since. We usually start prepping food on Wednesday for the Friday-night shindig. The Bear invites all the crews and drivers from the teams to come out, and he usually gets a pretty good turnout, about 300 people including some of the drivers. This is a full-blown deal complete with grilled chicken and venison, sweet corn, new potatoes, the works. It's usually 6 straight hours at the grill, but worth every bit of it.

Ain't Life Sweet Corn

Serves 6 'cause 1 ear is never enough!

Summer races are the perfect time to get sweet corn. And you can use your turkey fryer to boil it all!

1 Shuck corn and remove silk and excess stem. It helps to use a soft-bristle brush to remove the silk. Set corn aside but keep it chilled until you cook it.

2 Pour 2 gallons of water into your turkey fryer and crank it up. Add sugar and stir while water is heating. Just before the water starts to boil add the 3 tablespoons salt and corn. Place a lid on the pot and bring to a boil. Cook corn for 3 to 5 minutes. The corn should have a slight crunch to it! Don't overcook the corn!

3 Drain corn and place in a covered foil baking pan to keep it warm. Put softened butter on a plate and roll ears of corn in the butter. Salt and pepper to taste.

12	ears sweet corn
2	gallons water
1	cup sugar
3	tablespoons salt
½	cup butter, softened
	Salt
	Black pepper

Four-Leaf Clover

For some reason I have a knack for finding four-leaf clovers. Race day morning, in 1992 at The Glen, I was bent over a clover patch plucking out another one and stuffing it in my wallet. At the time there was a guy writing a book about Kyle Petty. We got to chatting and I walked back to the track with him so he could continue his interview about Kyle. He was jotting stuff down the whole time. Kyle went on to win the rain-shortened race that day, and somehow that little tidbit about the four-leaf clover ended up in the book.

Back End Broccoli Salad

Serves 4 to 6

I can't figure out why anyone wouldn't love broccoli. Maybe it's time one of our presidents tasted this dish.

1 Remove florets from broccoli stems and place in colander. Sprinkle salt over broccoli and place colander over a bowl to catch the liquid. Chill for 1 to 2 hours, allowing the water to drain. Keep the carrot, onion, radishes, and arugula chilled as well.

2 In a mixing bowl make the dressing by combining sour cream, cream cheese, peanut butter, olive oil, sesame seeds, water, and a pinch of salt. Whisk the ingredients together, adding more water if the dressing is too thick.

3 Give broccoli a quick rinse and shake or pat with paper towel as dry as possible. Place broccoli in a serving bowl and add the rest of the veggies; mix well. Coat with the dressing. Season to taste with salt and pepper.

2	small heads broccoli
1	tablespoon salt
1	carrot, peeled and shredded
1	sweet onion, diced
6–8	radishes, sliced into thin coins
1	cup arugula
3	tablespoons sour cream
2	tablespoons cream cheese, softened
1	tablespoon chunky peanut butter
1	teaspoon olive oil
1	teaspoon toasted sesame seeds
1	tablespoon water
	Salt
	Black pepper

One of my favorite places to visit while up at The Glen is Bully Hill Vineyards. Lillian Taylor, the owner, is a friend of "The Bear," so we always get treated like royalty when we go there for lunch. It's usually a table out on the balcony overlooking Keuka Lake near Hammondsport. Lunch starts with a few bottles of wine and an incredible appetizer, roasted garlic with goat cheese and toasted bread rounds. The view and the food are unbelievable. After lunch, we head over to the winery to taste some wine. They have nearly three dozen different types of wine to try. There's one for every taste.

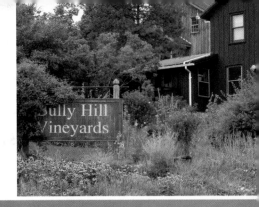

Racing Seasoned Rice Serves 6

First there's hunting season. Then the holiday season. Then the racing season. Now there's seasoned rice too!

1 Mix the rice, water, butter, salt (if desired), bouillon, onion, and garlic together in a large saucepan. Place the saucepan on the side burner and bring to a boil. Stir the ingredients once and place a tight-fitting lid on the pan. Reduce heat and simmer for 15 minutes. Remove from heat and let stand, covered, for another 10 to 15 minutes.

2   **cups uncooked rice (mix of Texmati white, brown, wild, and red)**

3   **cups water**

1   **tablespoon butter**

1   **teaspoon salt (optional)**

2   **chicken bouillon cubes**

2   **tablespoons dehydrated onion**

2   **teaspoons dehydrated garlic**

I'll Be Your Huckleberry

While at a race in Loudon, I met my buddy Mike from the No. 40 car for dinner at a joint in Weirs Beach. The waitress served us up a great meal and asked us if we wanted dessert. We were pretty stuffed, but I was all ears when she brought up blueberry pie. I asked her where the blueberries came from. She popped into the kitchen and came back a minute later with the answer. "They were picked from the wild in Maine," she says. So I tell her they're huckleberries. She replies, "Usually, most people don't call them that, but we do here." I had to give the pie a try, and it was just as good as Mom used to make it, trust me.

Wild Mountain Huckleberry Pie

Serves 8

I have my own secret huckleberry-picking grounds in the Poconos. If you can't find wild huckleberries, use fresh or frozen blueberries.

1 In a mixing bowl combine sugar, flour, cinnamon, and huckleberries. Place premade piecrust in a 9-inch pie pan. Crimp edges. Pour the berry mixture into prepared shell.

2 In another bowl mix the crumb topping. Combine flour and sugar. Mix well. Cut in chilled butter to make coarse crumbs. Sprinkle crumbs over the pie.

3 Preheat grill to 425°F. Place pie on upper cooking surface and close lid. Bake for 35 to 45 minutes. Remove the pie from the grill and let cool before serving. Serve with homemade whipped cream.

NOTE: To make the pie less runny, cut the sugar in the filling in half.

HINT: To keep the crust of the pie from browning too fast, wrap a 1-inch wide strip of foil around the edge of the crust. Remove 15 minutes before the pie comes out of the grill.

FOR FILLING:

1 cup sugar

5 tablespoons flour

½ teaspoon cinnamon

4 cups fresh huckleberries or blueberries

FOR CRUST:

1 premade piecrust

FOR TOPPING:

1 cup flour

½ cup sugar

½ cup butter, chilled

Homemade whipped cream

The Short Tracks

Bristol, Martinsville & Richmond

Short-track racing is where it's at. They say "rubbing is racing," but as far as I'm concerned, I say punting is racing! If a car is holding you back, just push 'em out of your way. You'll see more riled-up drivers at these three racetracks than in any big-city rush hour frenzy. A few red-hot temper tantrums make it all the more entertaining!

Bristol is the toughest ticket in town. This big bowl holds 160,000-plus seats, and they sell out every race. It's like a football stadium on steroids. The track itself has the steepest corners anywhere at 36 degrees. A half-mile lap in 15 seconds is the norm. Standing on pit road during a race is the noisiest thing you'll ever experience. The amount of carbon monoxide that settles to the bottom of the bowl will give you a headache to remember as well.

One restaurant near Bristol sticks out, The NASCAR Cafe in Johnson City. They've got one wall that is a replica of the track at Bristol with eight full-size race cars mounted on it. Of course the No. 3 is in the lead. It's a unique place for a race fan to check out.

Martinsville is known as the paper clip. The track is basically two drag strips connected by two tight corners. I like to call it "Spinsville." The action here is different from Bristol 'cause the crashes and spins usually take only a few cars out at a time. A caution here may not give you enough time to run to the restroom and back before restart.

When I'm not cooking, one of my hobbies is restoring antique Schwinn bicycles. I've found that Martinsville has some pretty good flea markets. During a racing weekend, I like to drop by a few places for a look, just in case someone is dumping an old Orange Crate or Lemon Peeler.

Richmond is a great place to see a race. The three-quarter-mile track offers up 2- and 3-wide racing. This track was originally a half-miler up until they expanded it in 1988. It turns out Richard Petty drove one of the bulldozers when they started the renovation. "The King" holds the record for the most wins at Richmond with 13. Maybe he took it personally enough to have a hand in building it to his own liking.

The tobacco industry has a rich history on the eastern seaboard and especially in Richmond. A great restaurant that reflects this heritage goes by the unlikely handle of The Tobacco Company. The building overflows with Victorian charm and flair. All quite proper and refined, you know. The decorations are from every corner of the United States. Warning: This one is not necessarily for the race fan on a budget.

You Did What?

I got to Bristol for the night race in 1986 and found out we had won the pole. That's always pretty good news on your team, no matter what. But then I heard something that I couldn't believe. I was talking to the head engine builder, and he told me he actually adjusted the engine so as not to have too much horsepower! Whatever he did worked. I guess sometimes to go fast you just have to slow down.

Four New Bologna Sandwiches
Serves 4

Bologna skins are tires on your car when they lose their tread. Racing tires come without tread. Now the recipe title makes sense!

1 Preheat grill to medium-high. Place a sheet of Reynolds Wrap Release foil on the grill surface with the "release" side up. Place butter on foil and reduce heat to medium. This will keep your bologna from slipping between the cracks in the grill.

2 Cut one slit from the center out to the edge of each bologna slice. Brown both sides in butter on the foil.

3 Build your sandwich on white bread with double layers of bologna and cheese (if desired). No self-respecting Southerner puts cheese on these things, but without it I find them a little plain. Use your favorite condiments, such as mayonnaise and mustard, to finish.

2   tablespoons butter

8   slices deli bologna, sliced
     $3/16$ inch to $5/16$ inch thick

8   slices white bread

8   slices sharp cheddar cheese
     (optional)
     Mayonnaise
     Mustard

Pig Out Pork Chops

Serves 8

The best tip I can give you about pork chops is don't overcook them. And serve them right when you pull 'em off the grill!

1 In a mixing bowl, combine bread crumbs, onion salt, and pepper. Mix thoroughly. Drizzle melted butter over crumbs and continue to mix until crumbs are evenly coated.

2 In a second mixing bowl whisk eggs. Place flour in a third bowl. Use the olive oil to coat two 11×15-inch baking pans. Make an assembly line of bowls in the following order: flour, eggs, and bread crumbs.

3 Run the pork chops through the assembly line of bowls. First coat the chops with flour, knocking off the excess. Then dip into egg batter and finish by coating the chops with the crumbs. Place 6 pork chops in each baking pan.

4 Preheat grill to 350°F. Place pans on lower cooking surface and bake for 40 to 45 minutes with lid closed, flipping the pork chops over after 20 minutes to achieve good golden color on each side and correct doneness.

2	cups Italian bread crumbs
2	tablespoons onion salt
1	tablespoon black pepper
1/4	cup melted butter, slightly cooled
4	eggs
1 1/2	cups flour
3	tablespoons olive oil
12	pork chops cut 3/4 inch thick, bone in

Brake This

One night in Richmond on the pace lap before the start of the race, Joe Nemechek's brake rotors were glowing cherry red. I asked Scott Eggleston, our crew chief, if he saw it, and he kind of nodded his head and said yes, he did. Next week I show up at the track, and I tell Scott I had some "real" brake ducts for the car, from someplace special. Of course, I got a totally confused look from him. I walked away and went to my truck and brought back some ductwork from a house I was working on. We're talking air-conditioning and heating ducts! I brought them into the garage, and he just busted up laughing.

Henry's Heart Attack Special

Serves 6

Henry Benfield and I made breakfast one morning for the Coors Light team. This is his concoction—cardiologists love him!

1 In a large skillet cook bacon on side burner. Remove bacon and place on a plate lined with paper towels to drain.

2 Start making toast in a toaster as you start cooking the eggs. Butter toast to taste. If you don't have a toaster, heat your grill to medium. Place bread on lower cooking surface and toast both sides.

3 On a side burner, heat a medium skillet to 300°F to 325°F. Pour enough oil in the pan to generously coat the bottom. Fry 2 eggs at a time in the oil, keeping a somewhat runny yolk. Season to taste with salt and pepper.

4 Assemble one sandwich at a time as the eggs come out of the pan. Start by stacking 2 eggs on a piece of toast, top with 2 to 3 slices of bacon, and finish with a slice of cheese. Spread mayonnaise to taste on the top slice of toast and place mayonnaise side down on sandwich.

1	pound bacon
12	slices wheat bread
¼	cup butter
2	cups Wesson oil
1	dozen eggs
	Salt
	Black pepper
6	slices medium-sharp cheddar cheese
	Mayonnaise

Texas Steakhouse & Saloon

In Martinsville, I always like to go to the Texas Steakhouse & Saloon. A strictly first-come, first-served kind of place. I got to know one of the waitresses pretty well, and she pulled strings to get the boys and me seated right away. Eventually, I could even call ahead, which wasn't one of their policies. One Friday after qualifying, I call her up and she holds a table for 10. We got there and the place was packed. Some of the other teams showed up right from the track. But we walked in and sat right down. The other teams were still standing when we were done. It really pays to be nice and tip well.

Bumpin' & Bangin' Wings
Serves 6

Good wings take time, but these are totally worth it. Don't freak out about all the hot pepper; it cooks off. People go crazy for these.

1 Combine crushed red pepper flakes, cayenne pepper, black pepper, and salt in a bowl and mix together. Lightly sprinkle one side of the wings with this seasoning blend.

2 Preheat grill to medium-high and place wings seasoned sides down on the grill. Sprinkle additional seasoning on the top side, reduce heat to medium, and close lid. Cook, turning several times, until golden brown. This takes about 20 to 30 minutes.

3 In a large stainless-steel mixing bowl combine brandy and chipotle sauce. Remove cooked wings from grill and coat generously with sauce. Put wings back on grill and cook for another 10 minutes, uncovered. Turn frequently to keep the sauce from burning.

4 Serve with celery sticks, carrot sticks, and dressings.

HINT: I buy large 2-packs of the raspberry chipotle sauce at Costco when I'm in Phoenix because sometimes I have a hard time finding it in my neck of the woods. You can buy it online too.

¼	cup crushed red pepper flakes
3	tablespoons cayenne pepper
1½	tablespoons black pepper
1	tablespoon salt
3	pounds fresh chicken wings
½	cup blackberry brandy
1	10-ounce jar or bottle raspberry chipotle sauce
6	stalks celery, cut into 3-inch sticks
4	carrots, peeled and cut into 2½-inch sticks
1	cup ranch dressing
1	cup blue cheese dressing

You're Kidding, Right?

Being a roadie in this three-ring racing circus has its stumbling blocks sometimes. In the late 1980s I usually didn't need to show up until race day. So one year I drove to Richmond and went into the office to get my credentials. Carl Hill, the person signing us in back then, looked up at me and kind of snickered, "Oh, I see no one bothered to tell you." I say, "Tell me what?" He says, "Your driver, Kyle, didn't even qualify! You made the trip for nothing!" He thought that was pretty funny. Then he went and told me that "The King," Richard Petty, didn't make the show either. Now that was big!

Spineless Boneless Pork Loin   Serves 6 to 8

One year I held culinary school and taught Michael Waltrip's and Bill Elliott's cooks how to make this recipe.

1 Rub the all-purpose seasoning without salt and the pepper on meat side of pork. Squeeze lemon on fat side of pork and rub in. This will help keep the fat from flaring up during cooking, but keep a spray bottle nearby just in case. Rub salted seasoning on the fat side of the pork.

2 Preheat grill to high. Place pork fat side down on lower cooking surface, close lid, and reduce heat to medium-high. Cook for 7 to 10 minutes. Staying next to the grill is a must to put out the occasional fire! Turn the meat once the fat side is golden brown. Reduce heat to medium, and if you have a three-burner grill turn off the middle burner. Place meat in the center of the grill. Maintain a temperature of 300°F to 350°F for about 1 hour. Check temperature with meat thermometer. The pork is ready when the thermometer reads between 140°F and 145°F.

3 Remove the meat from grill and let rest on a cutting board for 10 to 15 minutes. Cut pork in ½-inch slices.

HINT: An instant-read thermometer works great for this recipe.

2	tablespoons salt-free all-purpose seasoning
1	tablespoon black pepper
1	6- to 8-pound whole boneless pork loin
1	small lemon, cut in half
1	tablespoon with-salt all-purpose seasoning

Parts Are Parts

One February in Richmond, when it was still the old fairgrounds half-mile track, I was working for James Hylton. We discovered that one of the brake lines was bad. James told me to go into town and get a new one. I wondered what kind of place carries racing parts in town? Well, in those days, our cars really did use some off-the-shelf parts. So sure enough, I went to this place called Hones & Eanes. I bought all the brake lines they had on the rack and shot right back to the track. We didn't miss a lap of practice.

Garlic Smashed Potatoes

Serves 8 to 10

If you're feeding Coxey's Army, you're gonna need 5 pounds. If the army doesn't show, 5 pounds is still a good amount!

1 Take the heads of garlic and cut the tops off to expose the cloves. Drizzle 1 teaspoon of olive oil on the top of each head, lightly salt, and wrap in heavy-duty foil. Bake on grill with lid closed at 300°F to 325°F for 45 to 60 minutes.

2 On the side burner boil the potatoes in a large stockpot. Cook about 20 minutes or until fork-tender. Drain most of the water, leaving about 1 cup in the bottom of the pot.

3 Unwrap the cooked garlic and squeeze all the goodies from the root end into the pot of spuds. Add butter, milk, and cream. Mix with hand mixer or hand masher. (Hint: It helps if the butter is softened and the milk and cream are warm.) Add more milk, cream, and butter, if necessary. Season with salt and pepper to taste.

4 Place potatoes in foil roasting pan and cover with foil until ready to serve. An optional way to serve these is to take a fork and make ½-inch corn rows in potatoes. Double up the foil pan to prevent burning the bottom. Top with cheddar cheese and bake, covered, for an additional 10 minutes on the grill with lid closed at medium-low.

3	heads garlic
3	teaspoons olive oil
	Salt
5	pounds all-purpose potatoes, peeled and quartered
½	cup butter
½	cup whole milk
½	cup heavy cream
	Salt
	Black pepper
2	cups shredded cheddar cheese

Plug-Check Shrimp

Okay, a little mechanic lesson first. One way to check how your car is running is to take the car full out, then check the spark plugs. If they come back black, you're too rich with your fuel-to-air ratio. If they're white, you're too lean. If they're golden, you're just right. Shrimp are similar—they're dark if they're not done and nice and pink when they are. A restaurant in Martinsville delivered shrimp that were striped dark and pink. We found out the cook turned off the grill while they were cooking, so only the parts touching metal were cooked! Of course we had to send them back, but we have called them Plug-Check Shrimp ever since.

The Doc's Grilled Carrots
Serves 4 to 6

Hey, Kyle, you've got some up doc on your shirt. What's up, doc? Nothing, you silly wabbit. Kyle Petty falls for it every time.

1 Tear a piece of foil to make a 12×12-inch sheet. Place half of carrots on foil sheet. Drizzle half of olive oil over carrots and season with salt and pepper. Close up to make a packet. Repeat with remaining carrots.

2 Preheat grill to medium and place packets on lower cooking surface. Close lid and bake for 35 to 50 minutes, depending on carrot size. Remove carrots from packets and place directly on grill to make grill marks. Finish cooking directly on the grill for about 5 to 10 minutes more.

3 Place on serving platter and dot with butter.

1	pound whole carrots, peeled
¼	cup olive oil
	Salt
	Black pepper
¼	cup butter

My Garden

One September in Martinsville I made fresh cucumber salad. Sterling Marlin walks in the hauler and asks, "Hey, Big John, where did you get the cucumbers for this?" I replied (cool as a cucumber, of course), "Obviously you didn't know this, but I'll fill you in on a little secret. When we visit here in the spring, I always plant a garden outside turn 3. A couple of the locals peek in on it now and then to be sure it's getting enough water. And now, everything's ready to be picked." You talk about the deer-in-the-headlights look! I can't even remember how long it took before he figured I was pulling his leg.

Turn 3 Cucumber Salad
Serves 6 to 8

Fresh salads are great at the track. This is one of my favorites. Sterling Marlin likes it too! Just don't tell him where I get my cukes.

1 Wash cucumbers and cut the tips off each end. Use a vegetable peeler to stripe the cucumbers with ½-inch stripes. To do this, peel a ½-inch strip, then rotate cucumber and leave a ½-inch strip of skin. Repeat the process until all cucumbers are striped. Cut striped cucumbers into ⅛-inch- to ¼-inch-thick coins.

2 In a stainless-steel mixing bowl place cucumbers, onion, peppers, and spice. Mix thoroughly. Fold sour cream into mixture. Add black pepper to taste. Chill in bowl covered with plastic wrap for at least 1 hour. Add salt just before serving. Salt makes the sour cream dressing runny.

HINT: This is a good recipe to make ahead of time at home.

6	large firm cucumbers
1	large yellow onion
1	small green bell pepper, seeded and diced
1	small red bell pepper, seeded and diced
1	teaspoon salt-free Cajun spice
3	cups sour cream
	Black pepper
	Salt

Don't Try This at Home

I gotta fess up. The recipe on this page was supposed to be deep-fried ice cream. But when I was working on the recipe, seems we over-froze the ice cream using dry ice. There was no way we could cut it. We were at the track and our neighbor walks over and tells us he has a Sawzall cordless saw. Now, I'm a carpenter and use that tool to cut through pipe and concrete, so it seemed like a bit of overkill. Still, we tried it and dang if it didn't take three of us to get the ice cream sliced! And when we dropped it into the oil, it darn near blew up. I thought that you didn't need the hassle, but we laughed about what happened for hours!

On the Grill Cookies & Ice Cream
Serves 6 to 8

Your grill works as an oven too—perfect for baking cookies.

1 In a mixing bowl blend softened butter, brown sugar, and granulated sugar. Add eggs one at a time and blend in. Add vanilla and blend again. In a separate bowl mix together the flour, baking soda, and salt. Mix dry mixture into the butter and egg mixture. Stir in chocolate chips and nuts.

2 Make golf ball-size cookie balls from the dough. Place dough balls on a large ungreased cookie sheet, giving each cookie a 4×4-inch area for baking. Use the palm of your hand to flatten dough out to about ¼ inch thick.

3 Preheat grill to 375°F. Place cookie sheet on upper cooking surface and close lid. Bake for 7 to 9 minutes. Turn pan halfway through cooking.

4 Place 2 cookies and 3 big scoops of your favorite ice cream in each serving bowl while cookies are still warm.

Hint: Dry ice will keep your ice cream frozen in your cooler. But don't store dry ice in your freezer; dry ice will screw it up!

1	cup butter, softened
¾	cup brown sugar, packed
¾	cup granulated sugar
2	eggs
1	teaspoon vanilla extract
2¼	cups flour
1	teaspoon baking soda
1	teaspoon salt
2	cups chocolate chips
1	cup hickory nuts, chopped
½	gallon of your favorite ice cream

The Great Lakes

Chicago, Michigan & Indianapolis

The Great Lakes—big water, bratwurst, farmland, the Blues Brothers, Motown, names that end in *ski* and three superspeedways, including the most sacred of all racing grounds, the Indianapolis Motor Speedway!

Chicagoland has an odd shape about it. There's not one spot on the track that a driver can call a straightaway—it's just one constant corner. Anybody referring to a "backstretch" must need a chiropractor.

Chicago has so much to do that the choices are endless. If my boys in blue are in town, I head to Wrigley and catch a baseball game! If you make it to the waterfront downtown, check out the Sky Bar at the top of the Hancock building. The views from the 96th floor will give you acrophobia—or just the heebie-jeebies. Get there early so you can get a table by the window. Even the women's bathroom stalls have window views (so I'm told!). Prepare yourself for the elevator: 96 floors in 30 seconds! Pedal to the metal.

What can I say about the Indianapolis Motor Speedway? This is the granddaddy of all racetracks! I got goose bumps the first time I walked out on pit road. Stock car racing came to Indy for the first time in 1994. We almost won the Brickyard 400 the following year, if it hadn't been

for a blown left front tire in turn 4. Losses fade fast here; it's really kind of a religious experience. One of the cooler things to do at Indy is play a round of golf at the Brickyard Crossing Golf Course. I'd use the 14-day-advance tee time for race weekends if you want to get in. Four of the holes are in the infield of the racetrack. No. 16 is the signature hole on the course. The creek will get you every time!

Michigan is the original 2-mile, D-shaped oval. It's off in the "Irish Hills," which could easily be confused with the lake-riddled farmlands of southern Michigan. This area is normally covered by snow half of the year and the people are proud of it. Crank up the snowmobiles! Most of the teams stay in Ann Arbor for races here. There's a lot of restaurants downtown, but good luck finding parking! On Friday night there's a great all-you-can-eat fish fry at the Polar Bear restaurant in Clinton on Route 12. Just look for the penguin out front—he's the only one who is formally dressed.

St. Elmo Steakhouse

I've been chasing this racing three-ring circus for more than 25 years. One of the benefits is getting to try out restaurants across the country. I've been to some dives and to some top-notch places. St. Elmo Steakhouse is one of the top-notch ones. When you're out for the Brickyard 400 at Indianapolis and ready to splurge, this is the joint to check out. On race weekends you're bound to run into some of the big names. Like me, they come here for the famous shrimp cocktail and unbelievable steaks. I recommend the filet mignon along with a bottle of wine from the award-winning wine list.

Holy Cow Ribeyes & Spuds
Serves 6

I prepare this for the boys changing the tires. They shovel the stuff down like they're never gonna eat again!

1 Get your butcher to cut ¾-inch-thick ribeyes.

2 Mix the olive oil, steak marinade (this sauce is very potent and salty, so use more or less to suit your taste), garlic, and a few good turns of the pepper mill. Pour the marinade into a nonreactive plastic container. Place steaks in the marinade and refrigerate 4 to 24 hours.

3 Wrap the potatoes in aluminum foil. Preheat the grill to 350°F. Bake the potatoes on the grill for 1 to 1¼ hours. Unwrap them for the last 10 to 15 minutes. Place potatoes in an aluminum pan and cover with foil to keep warm while you grill the steaks. Serve potatoes with butter, grated cheddar cheese, and sour cream when steaks are done.

4 To cook steaks: Heat your grill wide open for about 10 to 15 minutes. Place steaks on grill. For the first 4 to 5 minutes leave them alone. Then turn them a quarter-turn and continue cooking for 3 to 4 minutes. Then flip 'em over and brush once with the marinade to finish them off. Serve medium to medium rare (145°F to 160°F). Watch out for flare-ups because the grill is really hot on this one.

6	¾-inch-thick ribeye steaks
1½	cups olive oil
3–4	tablespoons Dale's steak marinade
6–7	cloves garlic, finely minced Black pepper
6	russet baking potatoes
½	cup unsalted butter
8	ounces grated cheddar cheese
16	ounces sour cream

Roadkill Cafe

When two of my favorite things collide, cars and deer, it's usually pretty devastating to both parties. In Michigan alone there are more than 60,000 car/deer collisions every year. It makes me sick to see the deer go to waste, so I'm on three different police call lists if a deer gets hit by a car. I usually get five or six calls every fall to pick up a roadkill. A couple of years ago we made 150 pounds of jerky and fed it to the boys at the track. Some of it was from roadkills, so I tell the guys, "If you get a Chevy grille fragment, just spit it out. It won't hurt you!"

Ground Venison & Shells
Serves 6

I love using deer meat. I think venison tastes better than beef. But you can substitute ground beef if you want.

1 On the side burner boil pasta al dente (firm, not soft or mushy) according to package directions. Drain immediately.

2 On the side burner saute onion and garlic in olive oil in large saucepan over medium heat. Add ground venison, salt, and pepper and cook until meat is browned.

3 Once meat is done, drain any excess fat and add your favorite tomato sauce. Heat all the way through.

4 Mix the meat sauce and the drained shells in a large pot and it's ready to serve!

1	pound medium-size shell pasta
1	onion, chopped
3	cloves garlic, minced
2	tablespoons olive oil
2	pounds ground venison or lean ground beef
1–2	teaspoons salt
	Black pepper
1–2	16-ounce jars homemade or purchased tomato sauce

Something's Fishy

Most fish is too delicate to just throw on a hot lower grill surface. What I like to do is prepare a foil packet for the fish to kind of bake and steam it all at once. It's very easy to do and it doesn't take a lot of time. When I prepare a fish recipe that needs to be grilled, I use an extra gadget. It's a flat porcelain tray with small holes in it so that my fish won't stick, crumble, and fall through the grill racks.

Yeah, I Caught 'em Grilled Trout
Serves 6

The trick to this recipe is to make sure you catch enough trout! If you have to buy some at the store, just don't tell anyone.

1 Season the inside of the trout with a pinch of sea salt, pepper, and your favorite salt-free Cajun seasoning.

2 Tear heavy-duty foil into 6 pieces that are large enough to enclose each fish. Place each fish on half of each piece of foil and add 1 tablespoon oil, about a tablespoon of butter, and some onion slices on top. Squeeze a few drops of lemon juice on each fish and close up the foil.

3 Preheat grill to medium or medium-high for 10 to 15 minutes. Place fish on the grill and bake for about 15 to 20 minutes.

6	1-pound trout, cleaned and de-gilled
	Sea salt
	Black pepper
	Salt-free Cajun seasoning
6	tablespoons olive oil
½	cup unsalted butter
1	Vidalia onion, sliced into rings
1	lemon, cut in half

Dine'n and Dash'n

While at Michigan, I was having dinner with team owner Felix Sabates and the crew at a nice restaurant. We finish eating and make our way out to the parking lot when all of a sudden we're confronted by a half-dozen police officers with hands on their weapons. Felix starts to walk toward the cops and question what's going on and they yell to stay back. One cop says someone reported we didn't pay for our meal. While all this is going down I hear some laughing behind me. I turn around to see Jimmy Spencer and Junior Johnson busting up. Turns out they were the ones who had called the cops!

Teach Those Brats a Lesson
Serves 6

The trick to bratwurst is to boil them in beer before you grill 'em.

1 In a large saucepan on the side burner melt the butter and add the onions, bell peppers, cherry pepper, and banana pepper. Cook over medium heat for 15 minutes, stirring occasionally, to caramelize the onions and peppers.

2 Preheat the grill to medium. Place the caramelized onions and peppers in a small aluminum pan and add the marinara sauce to the mix. Place pan on the upper cooking surface of the grill to simmer.

3 Place a large pot on the side burner. Fill the pot with the beer; add bratwurst. Boil on high for about 10 to 15 minutes. After boiling, finish the brats off on the grill. Use the top shelf and brown for 10 to 15 minutes. Use tongs to turn brats so you don't puncture them and burn them with their own juices.

4 After you transfer the brats to the grill, it's time to warm up the sauerkraut. Put the sauerkraut in a saucepan on the side burner over medium heat.

5 Wrap the rolls in aluminum foil and warm them on the top shelf of the grill.

6 Choose your favorite topping and have at it!

¼	cup unsalted butter
2	onions, thinly sliced
2	red bell peppers, seeded and thinly sliced
1	cherry pepper, thinly sliced
1	banana pepper, thinly sliced
1	8-ounce jar marinara sauce
3	12-ounce cans beer
12	bratwurst
1	10-ounce jar sauerkraut
12	Italian rolls, split

Lou Malnati's Pizza

When you go to Chicago you've got to have a deep-dish pizza. If you don't have time to make one on the grill, I recommend Lou Malnati's. There are locations all over Chicago. The signature pie on the menu is the "Lou," a pizza so good they gave it his name. This thing comes with fresh spinach, mushrooms, and sliced tomatoes covered with a blend of mozzarella, Romano, and cheddar cheese. Order it with their world-famous butter crust. The coolest thing about the joint is that if you fall in love with their pie and you don't live in Chicago, don't worry. They'll FedEx you a frozen pie overnight that you can cook in your oven at home!

Think Deep-Dish Pizza
Serves 4

I know what you're thinking, pizza on a barbecue? Yes, indeed! And you can substitute any of your favorite ingredients.

1 Roll out the pizza dough on a clean surface. Before placing it in your largest deep skillet, sprinkle the bottom of the pan with a small amount of cornmeal. This will serve as the ball bearings to prevent the crust from sticking. Brush the olive oil on the sides of the pan to keep the dough from sticking to the sides as it rises.

2 Over medium heat, cook sausages. Use tongs when turning the links. Cut sausage into thin slices when done grilling.

3 Preheat grill to 400°F. While the grill is heating up, place the dough in the pan. Swirl on the pizza sauce with the back of a spoon. Layer the sausage, pepperoni, onion, and mushrooms on top of the sauce. Sprinkle mozzarella cheese over the top. Place pan on upper cooking surface of the grill and close the lid. Bake until crust is golden brown, about 15 minutes. Top with Parmesan cheese.

NOTES: Most supermarkets carry pizza dough in the refrigerator case, and they usually carry a good pizza sauce of their own brand as well. You also can get packaged grated Italian-blend cheese.

1–2	13.8-ounce cans pizza dough (depending on skillet size)
¼	cup cornmeal
2	tablespoons olive oil
2	12-ounce Italian sausages, mild or hot
1	15-ounce jar pizza sauce
4	ounces pepperoni, thinly sliced
1	small red onion, coarsely chopped
1	cup sliced mushrooms
1	pound mozzarella cheese, grated
	Parmesan cheese, grated

Need a Haircut?

One year, Kyle Petty was driving the No. 42 car and we had the car to beat at Indy. The drivers were putting the left side of the cars in the grass in the corners during that race. Sure enough, Kyle cuts a left front down in turn 4, plows the car into the wall, and takes out Sterling Marlin in the No. 4 car in the process. The safety crew starts to lift Kyle onto a stretcher and he screams so they put him back down. They try again and the same thing happens. This gets Sterling's attention. He checks with Kyle to see what's wrong and Kyle yells, "The guy is standing on my hair!" Every time they tried to lift him, they were pulling his hair out!

Pasta Salad
Serves 4 to 6

Make this ahead of time, store it in a plastic container, and chill it in your cooler. It's an incredible salad!

1 On the side burner boil pasta al dente according to package directions. Cool rapidly in ice water after boiling to avoid carryover cooking, then drain.

2 Whisk together olive oil, balsamic vinegar, and garlic in a small bowl. Set aside.

3 In a large bowl combine pasta, carrots, celery, onions, bell peppers, olives, and sun-dried tomatoes. Toss with dressing.

4 Just before serving, sprinkle with feta cheese and parsley. Season with salt and black pepper to taste.

1	pound bow tie pasta
½	cup olive oil
¼	cup balsamic vinegar
3–4	cloves garlic, minced
2	carrots, finely diced
2–3	stalks celery (including leaves), finely diced
1	medium red onion, diced
4–5	green onions, chopped
1	red bell pepper, diced
½	yellow bell pepper, diced
½	orange bell pepper, diced
½	cup black olives, pitted and sliced
1	cup oil-packed sun-dried tomatoes
8	ounces feta cheese, crumbled
¼	cup parsley, minced
	Salt
	Black pepper

The Farmer's Market

One of the great things about going to the races in Michigan is that it's summertime. All the local farmers have fresh vegetable stands alongside the country roads. You can usually get fresh sweet corn and other seasonal favorites near the track. There is a great farmer's market that I like to get my vegetables at when it's race weekend. It's in Jackson, about a half hour north of the speedway. The name of the market is Kuhl's Bell Tower Market, and it is on the corner of Louis Glick Highway and Mechanic Street in Jackson. This place is definitely worth the drive!

Totally Baked Onions
Serves 6

Stop crying. The onions are on the grill, so go cry about why you didn't win the race or something.

1 Peel onions and cut the root ends nice and flat. Cut out a ¼- to ½-inch-deep circle in the top of each onion. Rub butter over the outsides of the onions and lightly coat with sugar.

2 In a mixing bowl, combine Worcestershire sauce and garlic salt. Pour the sauce in the top of each onion. Wrap each onion in aluminum foil. Use a knife to cut a small hole in the top for steam to escape.

3 Preheat grill to medium. Place onions on lower cooking surface and close lid. Reduce heat to medium-low and bake for at least 1 hour. Unwrap and have at it.

Hint: For a different taste, put a teaspoon of brown sugar in each onion before baking.

6	large Vidalia onions
½	to 1 cup butter
1	cup sugar
½	cup Worcestershire sauce
1	teaspoon garlic salt

Dumpster Diving with Kyle

A few years ago I was cooking for Kyle Petty and the Coors Light team. After the race in Michigan, Kyle heads up to the hauler to snack on one of my pecan bars. When he gets there, he finds that the truck driver dumped the pecan bars in the trash by mistake! Kyle goes out back, digs 'em out of the bin, and eats them on the spot! A few years later, Kyle's walking through the garage when a fan comes up and says, "I know who you are." Kyle looks at the fan, and the fan says, "You're that guy who ate out of the trash can at Michigan!" He had no clue he was talking to Kyle Petty!

Dumpster Divin' Pecan Bars
Serves 12 to 16

Kyle Petty goes nuts for these. And did you know that Dumpster is a brand name? Learn something new every day.

1 Preheat grill to 350°F. Mix crust ingredients until crumbly then press into a pan (9×13×2 inches). Bake crust in grill 20 minutes or until golden brown.

2 While crust is baking, mix pecan filling ingredients until well blended. Spread filling evenly over hot crust. Bake for an additional 25 minutes or until set.

3 Cool on a wire rack, then cut into 2-inch squares. Makes about 30 bars.

FOR CRUST:

3	cups flour
½	cup sugar
1	cup margarine
½	teaspoon salt

FOR FILLING:

4	eggs, slightly beaten
1½	cups light or dark corn syrup
1½	cups sugar
3	tablespoons margarine, melted
2½	cups pecans, chopped

COMPETITION TIRE EAST

The Southern Beaches

Daytona & Homestead

Florida is a tropical paradise every way you turn, featuring beaches, the Keys, scuba diving, gators, swampland, hurricanes, retirees, spring break, fast boats, NASA, and NASCAR!

Ponce de León had no idea the land where he searched for the fountain of youth would be paved for racing. Born in 1959, Daytona International Speedway endured to become a signature venue for all stock car racing in the world. This 2.5-mile tri-oval track defines superspeedways and remains the prototype for every other tri-oval on the circuit. The Daytona 500 is the Super Bowl of stock car racing with a rich history of the weird and wonderful.

"The King," Richard Petty, holds the record with seven wins in the Daytona 500. In 1979 Donnie Allison crashed into Cale Yarborough coming to the checkers and Petty, a lap down at the time, wound up the winner. Rumor has it he is also the first and only driver to turn his Dodge into a bass boat by putting it squarely into Lake Lloyd. Even more dangerous than that trick was the time James Hylton's kid, Tweety, dumped a piranha in the lake. So much for swimming.

The most remarkable finish ever was when Petty and Pearson crashed coming to the checkers in 1976. One time Dale Earnhardt Sr. went on his lid, and after workers righted the car, he drove it back to the pits, only one lap down, and still finished.

The strangest race was when Cale Yarborough won the 500 with his team's show car that they had to snatch from downtown 'cause he'd wrecked all the other junk.

I really like the Charlie Horse Restaurant. It's the home of the all-you-can-eat crab legs. They consider closing the shutters when they see me coming because I once ate 21 platefuls of crab legs to drive off evil spirits before race day, but it worked. We won!

Homestead Miami Speedway was dedicated in 1995, three years after Hurricane Andrew permanently changed the neighborhood. Originally designed to be a miniature Indy, this island of asphalt in the Florida marshes was soon changed to be a flat oval and has now been renovated into a 20-degree, high-bank oval. Both its infield access tunnels are below sea level, and one of its two infield lakes is deep enough to submerge a six-story building. You know that's gotta hold a lot of bass.

If I find myself with some extra time, I like to visit the Keys. The world-class fishing is great, plus I can hop aboard my buddy Eric Bass' boat free of charge.

Taking One for the Team

Racing guys can be pretty superstitious. The night before we won our twin 125 qualifying race with Sterling, our team went out to dinner at the Charlie Horse Restaurant down in Daytona. They have this all-you-can-eat crab leg special. Let me tell you, when that restaurant saw me coming, you know they thought about closing up shop. Anyway, after 21 plates of three crab leg clusters each, I had all I could eat! The guys concluded that was why we won the next day. I've never been able to duplicate that luck again, but I've sure put away the crab whenever I go there!

Bay of Pigs Pulled Pork Sandwiches
Serves 8

A real roasting pan with a lid is best for this recipe.

1 Place pork in a heavy-duty roasting pan that can be covered with a lid. Sprinkle with brown sugar, celery salt, celery seed, onion salt, salt, and pepper. Add onion, celery, and ketchup directly on to the meat. Add tomato sauce and water to the bottom of the pan and cover with lid.

2 Preheat grill to 350°F. Place roaster on lower cooking surface. Close lid on grill and bake for 3 to 4 hours, checking every half hour for adequate moisture. Add water if necessary.

3 Remove the roaster from grill. Use forks to pull the meat apart. Add barbecue sauce to the pork and mix thoroughly. Serve on the Italian bread.

HINT: If you don't use a roasting pan, double up two foil pans with a little water between them, then cover with a foil lid.

4	pounds boneless pork loin (small end)
1/3	cup brown sugar, packed
1	teaspoon celery salt
1	teaspoon celery seeds
2	tablespoons onion salt
1	teaspoon salt
2	tablespoons black pepper
1	onion, chopped
1	stalk celery, diced
1/2	cup ketchup
1	8-ounce can tomato sauce
1	cup water
1/4–1/2	cup barbecue sauce (your favorite)
1	loaf Italian bread cut into 3/4-inch slices

Coming Through!

The trip to Daytona is a 14-hour drive down I-95 from my house. One trip was pretty quiet until I hit Jacksonville. I saw a couple of race team haulers on I-95 in front of me. There were cars full of fans dogging them, taking pictures, and screaming. I got close to the mayhem and saw that my pals Speedball and Catfish were the ones driving the trucks. Now, I'm tired and I've had enough of driving the double-nickel speed limit, so I take matters in my own hands, cut a path through the traffic, and open up the fast lane, getting the boys to follow me. I'm not going to say I was speeding, but we did get from Jacksonville to Daytona in 45 minutes!

Swimming to Freedom Swordfish

Serves 6

Swordfish should be firm, look good, and smell of fresh sea air.

1 Season each fillet with a pinch of salt and pepper on each side. Squeeze juice from the Key limes on the flesh side of the fillets, using ½ lime per fillet.

2 Preheat grill to medium-high and place fillets skin sides down on lower cooking surface. Close lid and reduce heat to medium. After 3 minutes pick up steaks and rotate 90 degrees to complete searing. After 2 more minutes flip steaks over and sear for another 2 minutes. Lift and rotate 90 degrees again and finish searing for about 1 minute.

6   ½-pound swordfish fillets
    Kosher salt
    Black pepper
3   Key limes, cut in half

That's a Big Fish

I like making mini-vacations out of race weekends. One time I got to Miami early for the race at Homestead to hang with my friend, Eric Bass. He happens to be a captain on a charter fishing boat. He took me and a buddy, Fred Peterson, out for a day of tarpon fishing. Fred was helping the No. 25 car with the tires that year. Fred ends up hooking a 100-pound tarpon on 20-pound test line. The fight was on for more than an hour. We finally got the fish in the boat, and it was longer than Fred is tall.

Didn't Make It to Freedom Swordfish

Serves 6

This is another delicious way to make a great swordfish fillet.

1 Season fillets with a pinch of salt and pepper on each side. Place fillets in a shallow dish. Pour fish marinade over fillets, cover, and let them marinate for 4 hours in the refrigerator.

2 Prepare a foil pouch using heavy-duty aluminum foil. Place fillets skin side down on foil. Top with 4 to 5 lemon slices and close aluminum foil pouch.

3 Heat grill to medium. Place foil pouch on cookie sheet and place on lower cooking surface. Close lid and bake for 20 to 30 minutes.

3 1-pound swordfish fillets
Kosher salt
Black pepper

1 bottle McCormick Golden Dipt lemon herb marinade or your favorite fish marinade

1 lemon, sliced

183

After winning the pole for the 500 at Daytona, our team owner, Felix Sabates, took the whole team out for a celebratory dinner at the Chart House. His yacht was anchored right next to the restaurant, so it was a quick walk over for him. The hostess just about fell over when she heard we had a reservation for 26! Well, we had a great dinner but, like it sometimes happens, it was probably a premature celebration. We truly had the car to win, until Kyle Petty got into a little fender bender with Bobby Hillin on race day. At least the dinner was good!

Just Junk Jerk Chicken
Serves 6

When a driver thinks his car isn't performing, he'll radio in and tell his crew chief that it's junk. This recipe is far from junk!

1 Combine jerk seasoning, thyme, onion powder, allspice, and orange juice in a small mixing bowl to make a paste. Rub paste generously on both sides of the chicken.

2 Preheat grill to medium-high. Place chicken on lower cooking surface and close lid. Reduce heat to medium. Cook chicken 6 to 7 minutes on each side or until thermometer reads 170°F.

3 Serve with quartered oranges.

HINT: For more kick, double the paste ingredients.

2	tablespoons McCormick Caribbean jerk seasoning
1/2	cup fresh thyme, chopped
2	teaspoons onion powder
1/2	teaspoon ground allspice
2	tablespoons fresh squeezed orange juice
6	large skinless, boneless chicken breast halves
6	oranges, cut into quarters

John Who?

I'm walking through the garage at Daytona during speed week one year when I hear someone yell, "John!" I turn around to see a guy, his wife, and their daughter. The chipmunks start turning in my head as I try to figure out where I know them from. They ask if we can all take a picture together and, of course, I gladly agree. We finish and he asks, "Aren't you glad football season is over with?" I'm thinking, sure, why not, so I say, "Sure am." As they walk away it all starts to click in my head. They thought they were getting a picture with John Madden!

Slice of Heaven Plantains
Serves 4 to 6

Forget the grill for this recipe. Pull out the deep fryer and taste these delicious banana-like treats.

1 Pour peanut oil into turkey fryer. Bring the oil up to a temperature of 400°F in the deep fryer. Lift basket out of oil and add plantain slices. Submerge the basket slowly in the oil. Cook until plantain chips are golden brown or begin to float, about 3 to 4 minutes.

2 Remove and place on plate lined with paper towels to drain. They don't get really crispy, but man, do they taste good! Season plantains with powdered sugar and salt.

1	gallon peanut oil or canola oil
6	large plantains, peeled and sliced ⅛ inch thick
½	cup powdered sugar
1	teaspoon salt

Daytona Victory Lane

On the eve before running our twin 125 qualifier at Daytona, our crew chief, Buddy Barnes, known as Red Dog, got the team together to discuss the next day's race strategy. After a long-winded affair, he ended by saying when we win our race not to celebrate too long because there was lots of work left to do on the car. Sure enough, we end up in victory lane. Red Dog is up with the spotters, so he can't even join in on all the fun, but he calls down and tells us to forget what he said earlier and have a good one. After going to Daytona for more than 16 years, it was my first time in victory lane there! Yeeehaaaa!

After the Race Fruit Salad
Serves 6 to 8

When tailgating at a race in the summer, nothing beats a cool treat. This one is kid friendly too.

1 Put blueberries, raspberries, blackberries, grapes, strawberries, apples, pineapple, bananas, and peaches in a stainless-steel mixing bowl. Squeeze the lime juice over all the fruit. Chill for at least 1 hour in your cooler or refrigerator.

2 Chill another stainless-steel mixing bowl and the whipping cream in the freezer, or on ice, for about 15 minutes. Remove from freezer and pour whipping cream into bowl. Whisk briskly until soft peaks form. Fold in the vanilla and powdered sugar. Taste to make sure it's sweet enough. Add more sugar, if necessary.

3 Serve fruit in dessert bowls and top with whipped cream.

1	cup blueberries
1	cup raspberries
1	cup blackberries
1	cup red seedless grapes
2	cups fresh strawberries, halved
2	apples, cored and cut into ½-inch slices
1	pineapple, cored, peeled, and cut into 1-inch slices
3	bananas, peeled and sliced
4	peaches, pitted and sliced
1	Key lime, halved
1	pint heavy whipping cream
1	teaspoon vanilla extract
½	cup powdered sugar

My New Girlfriend

One race at Daytona, Wynonna Judd happened to be in the garage. Sterling Marlin tells me to find her and bring her over to his motor coach to visit with his wife, Paula. Wynonna comes by our hauler, and I explain the situation and she says she's up to meeting Mrs. Marlin. When I start to lead the way, she grabs my arm and puts it around her. Now we're strolling through the garage arm in arm, and all the crew guys are looking at me like, "How in the heck do you know Wynonna?" You know, sometimes you just have to act like you know what you're doing and people will take your lead.

Life's a Beach Grilled Pineapple

Serves 8

Clean your grill surface thoroughly before you make this one. You don't want any Speedway Chicken flavoring your dessert!

1 Cut the bottom and the crown off the pineapples so you have a flat surface. Then cut off wide strips of the skin and remove the eyes. Cut the cleaned pineapple into quarters lengthwise. Cut the core out of each piece. Rub each quarter with olive oil and add a pinch of salt to each.

2 Heat grill to medium-high and place pineapple quarters on grill just long enough to make grill marks on all sides of the fruit (about 2 minutes per side). Do not cook through.

3 The fruit will have good-looking grill marks and will be warmed through. Serve on dessert plates with a sprinkle of brown sugar and two scoops of coconut ice cream.

4	fresh pineapples
4	tablespoons olive oil
1	teaspoon salt
½	cup brown sugar, packed
½	gallon coconut ice cream (or scoops of French vanilla ice cream rolled in shredded coconut)

That's a Pie Tree

Traveling back and forth from our hotel to the track in Homestead is a visual treat. There are lots of neat things to look at while on the road. One thing that sticks out are all the Key lime trees. Acre after acre. What's kinda unique about them is that the limes are yellow and not green. And man, they sure do make great pies! One day, I was driving one of the crew guys to the track and pointed to the trees and said, "That's a pie tree there." He looks and I tell him he missed it. "You gotta look fast," I tell him. "There's another one!" I think he's still wondering where those pies come from.

Checker Flag Key Lime Pie Serves 8

Make this at home, put it in a sealable pie container, and bring it with you in the cooler. No fuss or muss at the track!

1 In a mixing bowl beat the cream cheese with your mixer. Add condensed milk and mix well. Add lime juice and continue mixing. Pour mixture into a premade graham cracker crust. Refrigerate for at least 2 hours.

2 Chill a stainless-steel mixing bowl and the whipping cream in the freezer, or on ice, for about 15 minutes. Remove from freezer and pour whipping cream into chilled bowl. Whisk briskly until soft peaks form. Fold in the vanilla and powdered sugar. Taste to make sure it's sweet enough. Add more sugar, if necessary.

3 Cut pie into 8 slices and top with whipped cream.

1   8-ounce package cream cheese, softened

1   cup sweetened condensed milk (approximately 1 small can)

½   cup fresh Key lime juice (about 10 to 12 Key limes)

1   purchased 9-inch graham cracker crust

1   pint heavy whipping cream

1   teaspoon vanilla extract

½   cup powdered sugar

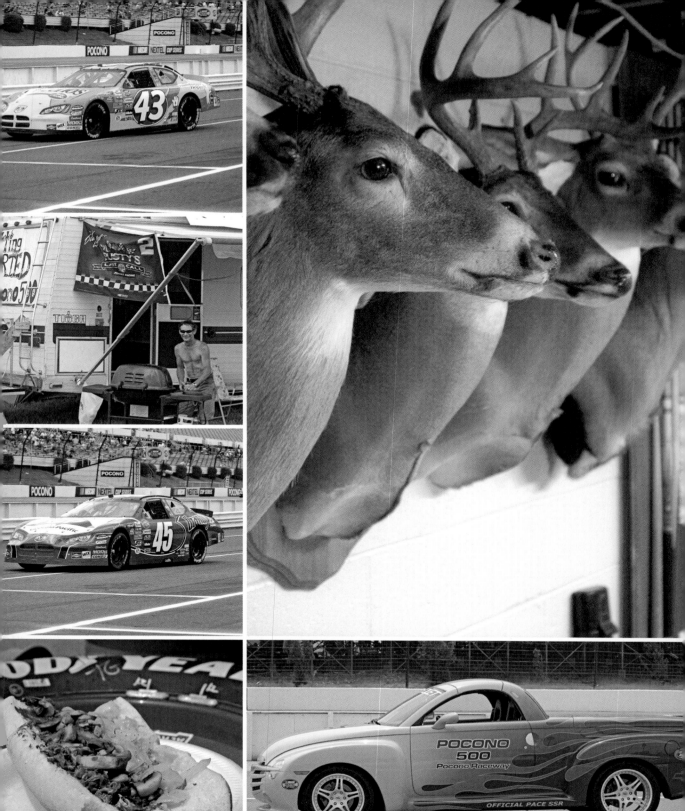

Big John's Country

Pocono & Dover

This is my country! Rolling hills, scenic river valleys from the Appalachian Trail to the Atlantic Ocean, and rival for the title "Honeymoon Capital of the World." The four "Rs" of my country are recreation, relaxation, romance, and racing. Oh yeah, I forgot rifles. Remember, I love to hunt!

It all started for me at a high-banked, 1-mile oval nicknamed "The Incredible Mile." Now, of course, it's "The Monster Mile." I would always go to the race at Dover and get a ticket from a scalper on race day for under face value … try doing that now! At one race I finally decided that I was on the wrong side of the fence and made my move. I got my first break in 1980 pitting a car for James Hylton at Dover, and the rest, as they say, is history. The place only seated about 26,000 back then. Now after 16 consecutive years of construction it seats more than 140,000 hungry racing fans.

"The Monster Mile" team hangout is at the Sheraton. You'll run into most of the crews there having a beer or two after practice and qualifying. Dover is only a stone's throw from Delaware Bay, which is known for its blue crabs. You can run down to the water with a chicken head on a string if you want, but I think the best place to get crab is Sambo's off Route 9. Sometimes a do-it-yourselfer ought to leave it up to the pros.

They call Pocono the superspeedway that drives like a road course. One of the unique things about Pocono is the wildlife—not the people, but the real animals that you can cook! Up until they fenced in the track it was not uncommon to have deer running across the back straightaways … yes, two of them. You see, the track is basically in the shape of a triangle, not an oval. Not to be outdone by Dover, Pocono had its own mere 10-year remodel and went from offering only 375 toilets to now a whopping 1,000 stalls.

The crowd at Pocono is one of the wildest on the circuit. If it rains over the weekend you'll probably find more than one muddy slip-and-slide with a half-naked mud fest at full throttle. The school bus-style motor homes rival even those that show up at Talladega—and that's saying something. I pulled up on race day last year at 5:30 a.m. and couldn't believe how many people were walking around with beer. I had to ask myself, "Did they just get up, or haven't they gone to bed yet?"

Shenanigans at Lake Harmony is about a half-hour drive from the track outside of Pocono. If you're looking for a good home-cooked meal, this is the joint to check out. Oh, and my private huckleberry stash is in the Poconos as well, but I'm not tellin' where … you'll just have to find your own.

The King and I

I have to admit I'm a big fan of "The King," Richard Petty. Of course, he was easy to like since he won quite often back in the day. I had the luck of seeing him win in person on several occasions when I was younger. During one race at Dover he was 13 laps down early in the race. Back then it was a 500-mile race instead of the 400-mile races of today. So I think he's junk, and I pack it up and head home. I turn the race on in the truck and can't believe what I hear. "The King" is making up laps! I was dumbfounded when he actually won the race. I never left a race early again!

It's Not Roadkill
Venison Backstrap

Serves 4

Dale Earnhardt Sr. loved this dish. I would always deliver a plate to him. He wouldn't say much, but boy, would he dig in!

1 Trim all silver skin and tallow from backstraps. In a mixing bowl combine the 3 cups oil through balsamic vinegar. Pour into a resealable plastic bag and place venison in bag. Marinate for 1 to 6 days in the refrigerator, shaking it up twice daily.

2 On the side burner of the grill place a large cast-iron skillet and heat to medium-high. Remove backstraps from marinade. Saute backstraps, using some of the marinade, medium-rare to medium, or to your liking. I like it just pink in the middle. Remove and place on platter. Let rest for 10 to 15 minutes.

3 Pour the red wine into the skillet and deglaze the browned bits in the bottom of the pan. Let this reduce to almost a glaze (it should coat the back of a spoon). Strain into a bowl. Make sure everything is out of skillet and add the 2 tablespoons olive oil; bring to a simmer and add the shallots. Saute shallots, then add back the strained liquid from the reduction. Reduce by half again. Add the 3 cups blackberry brandy and reduce to a glaze. Turn down heat; gently whisk in the butter.

4 Cut backstraps into ½-inch slices and place on a platter. Pour brandy glaze over the venison, reserving some for individual dipping.

2	6-inch venison backstraps
3	cups extra-virgin olive oil
6	cloves garlic, minced
3	tablespoons black pepper
½	large onion, chopped
2	bundles green onions, chopped
½	cup each fresh sage, thyme, rosemary, and parsley, chopped
2	tablespoons horseradish
2	tablespoons barbecue sauce
2	whole apples, thinly sliced
3	tablespoons applesauce
½	cup blackberry brandy
3	tablespoons balsamic vinegar
1	cup good red wine
2	tablespoons extra-virgin olive oil
4	shallots, finely diced
3	cups blackberry brandy
¼	cup butter, cut up

Deer Crossing

Years ago at Pocono, the late Neil Bonnett was driving for Junior Johnson in the No. 11 car. It's early in the practice session when Neil pulls the car back in the garage. I'm looking at the front of his car and there are four sticks coming out of the grille. I look closer and realize it's a small deer, and the sticks are its legs. By now everyone in the garage has come over to see what's going on. All I can hear is Junior Johnson screaming at Neil about wrecking the car. Neil fires back, "It just jumped out in front of me, what was I supposed to do?" I kept thinking to myself, "If this deer were a little bigger, we'd be having some venison for lunch!"

Fresh from the Forest Meat Loaf
Serves 4

As with all my venison recipes, you can substitute lean ground beef if your freezer is out of venison. Heaven forbid!

1 Mix ground venison, bread crumbs, eggs, salt, onion, pepper to taste, and condensed milk with an electric mixer or hand mixer. Mold into a greased loaf pan and transfer to a foil pan. Cover loaf with slices of bacon.

2 Preheat grill to 375°F. Place pan on lower cooking surface and bake with lid closed for 1¼ to 1½ hours.

Hint: If you use lean ground beef, mix with your hands, providing they're clean, of course!

2   pounds ground venison or lean ground beef
1   cup Italian-style bread crumbs
3   eggs
2   teaspoons salt
1   onion, finely chopped
    Black pepper
1   cup sweetened condensed milk (use ½ cup if you use ground beef)
4   slices bacon

What Race?

After James Hylton retired as a driver, he hired a Canadian, Trevor Boys, to drive the car. We were at Pocono running around 13th when Trevor comes in for a pit stop. I'm running around the front of the car to jack the left side up when I notice a beautiful brunette behind our pits. Trevor notices too. She's not wearing a shirt. Trevor forgets what he's doing. I drop the jack and the car just sits there. Finally, James starts pounding on the car to get Trevor going, with no success. Soon enough, some official asked her to put her top on, and escorted her from the track!

Say Cheese Steak Sandwiches Serves 6

The key to a great Philly cheese steak sandwich is the bread. I use Italian sub rolls from the Conshohocken Italian Bakery.

1 Place a griddle on the lower cooking surface of the grill. Heat griddle to high. Put oil and butter on griddle. Once butter is melted, lay out chipped steak on one side of griddle and the onion, bell and jalapeño peppers, and mushrooms on the other side. Season with salt and black pepper. As the chipped steak cooks, break it apart with two spatulas.

2 Once the veggies and steak are cooked, separate the steak into 6 bun-length servings. Spoon marinara sauce over meat. Top each portion with 3 slices of cheese. Split the Italian buns not quite all the way through and place facedown over each stack of meat and cheese. Let buns warm about a minute, then close buns and flip each stack over with a spatula. Place on a serving platter. Top with the grilled veggies.

4 tablespoons blended oil (30 percent olive oil, 70 percent vegetable oil)

¼ cup butter

3 pounds chipped steak

1 onion, sliced

1 cup bell peppers, thinly sliced

½ cup jalapeño peppers, thinly sliced

1 cup mushrooms, sliced

Salt

Black pepper

1 16-ounce jar marinara sauce

18 slices white American or provolone cheese

6 Italian sub rolls

Panties in a Bunch?

One race at Dover, Kyle Petty and Michael Waltrip were swapping paint all day long. This blossomed into a real good tussle on pit road after the race ended. I ran down to the melee and got in between them, keeping my back to Michael and pushing him away from Kyle. I don't even know why they had their dander up in the first place. I told everybody, "Looks like one chipped a nail and the other got a runner in his pantyhose!" My brother-in-law, Terry Davis, happened to be watching the race live at a bar in Louisiana when someone asks, "Who the heck is that big guy in between them?" Terry replies, "Aw shoot, that's my brother-in-law!"

Shoot the Bull
Pork & Sauerkraut

Serves 6 to 8

So easy, you'll have time to shoot the bull with friends.

1 Cut pork loin in half. Coat the fat on both pieces with the salt, then sprinkle with seasoned salt and pepper. Season with unsalted pork seasoning on the meat side of both pieces.

2 Heat large skillet to medium-high on side burner. Place both pieces of pork loin fat sides down in skillet. Cook fat until semi-crisp. Flip both loins over and brown the meat side. Remove from skillet and place in large foil roasting pan with the fat sides up. Pour 2 cups of the water in the pan and add onions. Cover with aluminum foil.

3 Preheat grill to 350°F. Place pan on lower cooking surface. Bake with cover closed for 1 to 1½ hours until center is 160°F. Remove from grill and place both loins on a serving platter to rest for 10 to 15 minutes.

4 Use a large saucepan on the side burner and add remaining ¼ cup water, sauerkraut, and apples. Bring to a simmer and heat through, approximately 25 minutes, stirring every 5 minutes.

5 Place cooked sauerkraut mixture in original roasting pan with onions and pork juices. Cut pork loin in ½-inch slices and lay over the sauerkraut.

1	5-pound boneless pork loin
5	tablespoons salt
	Seasoned salt
	Black pepper
	Salt-free pork seasoning
2¼	cups water, divided
2	medium onions, peeled and quartered
3	1-pound packages sauerkraut
3	Granny Smith apples, cored and quartered

Repeat

At the second race at Pocono in 2004, I was talking with one of the engine builders for the No. 48 Lowe's car. I asked if he'd seen the days TV listing? He said no, he hadn't. "The race has an R next to it in the paper," I joked. He says, "Rerun?" I reply, "No, repeat! You guys won the first race here this year, and I guess you're going to win it again today." Sure enough, Jimmie Johnson wins the race. The next year, I'm talking with Jimmie's guys at Dover. I told 'em again I'd see them in Victory Lane. Sure enough, they won Dover too. Is talking to me good luck or what?

Get a Grip
Grilled Asparagus

Serves 4

There's nothing better than a side of asparagus to liven up a main dish!

1 Snap one asparagus spear at the base, allowing it to break naturally as it bends. Place the shortened spear with rest of the bunch and use a knife to cut all of the spears to the same length.

2 Heat a large skillet on a side burner to medium; add olive oil and butter. Place asparagus in pan and saute until semisoft.

3 Add garlic and cook until the garlic is light brown. Squeeze lime over asparagus in pan, half a section at a time. Serve immediately.

1	pound asparagus
4	tablespoons extra-virgin olive oil
1	tablespoon salted butter
5	cloves garlic, minced
1	lime, cut in half

Who Put That Wall There?

During one race at Pocono when I was working on Sterling Marlin's team, we were running like junk. Nothing was going right at all. Then, about halfway through the race Sterling hits the wall in turn No. 3 and pancakes the right side of the car. But he didn't stop; he just kept on going. We're all wondering what's going to happen. Then he radios in a couple of laps later and tells us the car is running better after the scrape! We came in third that day, but I don't think he ever tried to fix a car that way again!

Something New Potatoes

Serves 4 to 6

You can use any type of potatoes you like, but I prefer little red potatoes.

1 Scrub red potatoes and cut in half. Pour most of the olive oil in a mixing bowl. Toss potatoes in oil to coat.

2 In a separate foil roasting pan pour the remaining olive oil and spread on the bottom of pan. Place the red potatoes in an even layer in the pan. Sprinkle with garlic, paprika, and salt to taste. Cover pan with aluminum foil.

3 Preheat grill to 350°F. Place pan on bottom cooking surface and bake for 1 hour with grill cover closed. After 1 hour remove aluminum foil and sprinkle chives over potatoes. Continue cooking, uncovered, for 15 minutes with grill cover closed.

18 small red potatoes
¼   cup extra-virgin olive oil
8   cloves garlic, minced
1   tablespoon paprika
    Salt
1   bunch chives, finely chopped

My First Chance

The first team I worked on was owned and driven by James Hylton. We were in Dover during the 1980 season when he asked me to be the jack man at the race. I jumped at the opportunity. The first pit stop comes, and when I'm jacking the left side of the car, it slips. So I brace the jack by placing my knee and foot between the jack and the pit wall. I thought my career was gonna be over before it started. The stop went off without a glitch. After the race, James told me I was the best jack man he had ever had. I sure felt lucky.

Gas Man's Butternut Squash

Serves 4

One thing most people overlook when grilling is doing something tasty with veggies. This one adds a nice surprise to the party.

1 Cut squash in half. Use a spoon to scoop out the seeds and membrane from the center of each squash. Rub olive oil on the inside of each half and season with salt, pepper, and garlic powder. Marry the halves back together and wrap tightly in heavy-duty aluminum foil.

2 Preheat the grill to 325°F. Place the squash standing up on the lower cooking surface and bake with the lid closed for 1¼ hours. Lay squash down and cook on each side for another 5 minutes per side.

HINT: For an extra treat, put a dollop of butter and brown sugar in the hollowed out part before serving.

2   butternut squash
½   cup extra-virgin olive oil
2   teaspoons kosher salt
     Black pepper
     Garlic powder (use no more than ¼ teaspoon per half)

Wild Huckleberries

There's nothing better than wild huckleberries. They are actually wild blueberries. Making pies and breads with them can make you look like you actually know what you're doing because they're so good! Mike Motil, the tire specialist on the No. 40 car, introduced me to his parents who live in West Hazelton, Pennsylvania. Joe, his dad, and I try to make an annual event of picking this honey hole in the Poconos. We usually get 10 to 12 quarts of berries every year. Don't ask me where it is, and don't try to follow me there either. All I'll give is my rank and serial number!

Blueberry Bandana Bread
Serves 4 to 6

At the end of the weekend, there's usually some black bananas left around. I'll collect them up and make this.

1 Place butter and sugar in mixing bowl and blend until creamy. Add eggs and vanilla. Add flour, baking soda, and salt; mix well. Stir in bananas, blueberries, and walnuts. Pour mixture into a greased 9×5-inch loaf pan.

2 Preheat grill to 350°F. Place pan in the center of the lower cooking surface. Turn middle cooking element off. Bake with grill lid closed for 50 to 60 minutes. Test doneness in the middle of the loaf with wire cake tester. If it comes out clean, the bread is done. Cut into ½-inch slices.

½   cup butter, softened
1   cup sugar
2   eggs
1   teaspoon vanilla extract
1½ cups flour
1   teaspoon baking soda
½   teaspoon salt
2   large ripe bananas, mashed
1½ cups fresh blueberries
¾   cup walnuts, chopped

RESOURCES

Arizona Brand Tortillas
If you want to taste the difference, here's how to find out where they're sold nearest you.
3121 West Washington Street
Phoenix, AZ 85009
(602) 273-7139

McCormick Montreal Seasonings
These should be easy to find, but these online folks sell them too.
espicebazar.com
AASpices.com

Crawfish
OK, they are kind of hard to find. But if you really want a treat, you can order bushels of the little guys and have them shipped in live!
www.cajuncrawfish.com
www.klcrawfishfarms.com
www.shrimpshrimp.com

Dale's Steak Seasoning
This can be tricky to find. You can use your favorite steak sauce or you can get it online from Dale's.
www.dalesseasoning.com

Mrs. Dash Chicken Seasoning
I love this salt-free stuff. If you can't find it at the store, check out the Mrs. Dash website and order it.
www.mrsdash.com

Paul Prudhomme's Vegetable Magic
This mix of spices is amazing. Use it on dang near anything. I even like it in my eggs!
www.chefpaul.com

Raspberry Chipotle Sauce
If you can't find it at Costo, they have some good brands online here.
www.sauceco.net

Sweet Baby Ray's Barbecue Sauce
You can order direct from the source!
Phone: (877) 729-2229

Texas Pete's Hot Sauce
You can use your favorite hot sauce, but if you want to taste it my way, these folks sell it online. Just visit their website and go to product index and look it up by name.
www.salsasetc.com

Tony Chachere's Original Creole Seasoning
You just gotta try this stuff! You can buy it online at this website if you can't find it at your supermarket.
www.tonychachere.com

Tony Stewart's "Smoke" Bar-B Que Sauce
I love helping friends and when they have great food to sell, you can count me in! You can find Tony's tasty sauce at his online store.
www.tonystewartstore.com

Venison
Yes, you can substitute beef! But why would you want to?

Zatarain's Products
From crawfish boil to great rice, this stuff is the real deal. I order it from the source and keep it handy.
www.zatarain.com

PLACES TO VISIT

Bully Hill Vineyards
I love going here—I hope you do too!
8843 Greyton H. Taylor Memorial Drive
Hammondsport, NY
(607) 868-3610
www.bullyhill.com

Charlie Horse Restaurant
810 S. Atlantic Ave.
Ormond Beach, FL 32176
www.charliehorserestaurant.com
(386) 672-4347

Gundlach Bundschu Winery
2000 Denmark St.
Sonoma, CA 95476
www.gunbun.com
(707) 938-5277

The Inland Reef
If you see Georgie, let him know Big John sent you!
500 Hamilton Street
Geneva, NY
(315) 789-2704

Jackson-Kuhl's Bell Tower Market
This is a really great place & it's only 30 minutes from the track. Call to be sure they're open because it's a seasonal market.
117 Louis Glick Highway
Jackson, MI
(517) 782-9011

Los Dos Molinos
Hot and tasty!
8646 S. Central Avenue
Phoenix, AZ
(602) 243-9113

Lou Malnati's Pizza
I dream of this stuff and they deliver anywhere! They have lots of locations in Chicago, so check out their website.
www.loumalnatis.com
(800) LOU-TO-GO

Palms Casino Resort
Ghostbar (55th Floor)
4321 W. Flamingo Rd.
Las Vegas, NV 89103
www.palms.com
ghostbarreservations@palms.com
(702) 942-7777

Pee Dee's Farmer's Market
I love this market—don't tell my neighbors that it's where I get my spring flowers!
2513 W. Lucas Street
Florence, SC
(843) 665-5154

Sambo's Tavern
283 Front St.
Leipsic, DE 19901
(302) 674-9724

Saylors Landing
305 Harbor Dr.
Sausalito, CA 94965
(415) 332-6161

St. Elmo Steak House
I think this is one of the best places anywhere to get a truly great steak.
127 South Illinois Street
Indianapolis, IN
(317) 635-0636
www.stelmos.com

Texas Steakhouse & Saloon
I'm telling you—if you're not going to cook it, come here!
283 Commonwealth Blvd.
Martinsville, VA
(540) 632-7133
www.texassteakhouse.com

Victory Junction Gang Camp
4500 Adam's Way
Randleman, NC 27317
www.victoryjunction.org
(336) 498-9055
1 (877) VJC-CAMP

DIRECT GRILLING FISH AND SELLFISH*

FORM OF FISH	THICKNESS, WEIGHT, OR SIZE	GRILLING TEMPERATURE	APPROXIMATE TIME	DONENESS
Fillets, steaks, cubes (for kabobs)	½ to 1 inch thick	Medium	4 to 6 minutes per ½-inch thickness	Flakes
Shrimp (for kabobs)	Medium (41 to 50 per pound) Jumbo (20 to 21 per pound)	Medium Medium	5 to 8 minutes 7 to 9 minutes	Opaque Opaque

INDIRECT GRILLING FISH AND SELLFISH*

FORM OF FISH	THICKNESS, WEIGHT, OR SIZE	GRILLING TEMPERATURE	APPROXIMATE TIME	DONENESS
Fillets, steaks, cubes (for kabobs)	½ to 1 inch thick	Medium	7 to 9 minutes per ½-inch thickness	Flakes
Shrimp (for kabobs)	Medium (41 to 50 per pound) Jumbo (20 to 21 per pound)	Medium Medium	8 to 10 minutes 9 to 11 minutes	Opaque Opaque

* All cooking times are based on fish removed directly from refrigerator.

DIRECT GRILLING PORK*

CUT	THICKNESS/ WEIGHT	GRILLING TEMPERATURE	APPROXIMATE TIME	DONENESS
Chop with bone (loin or rib)	¾ to 1 inch 1¼ to 1½ inches	Medium Medium	11 to 13 minutes 16 to 20 minutes	160°F medium 160°F medium
Chop (boneless top loin)	¾ to 1 inch 1¼ to 1½ inches	Medium Medium	7 to 9 minutes 14 to 18 minutes	160°F medium 160°F medium

INDIRECT GRILLING PORK*

CUT	THICKNESS/ WEIGHT	APPROXIMATE TIME	FINAL GRILLING TEMPERATURE (when to remove from grill)	FINAL DONENESS TEMPERATURE (after 15 minutes standing)
Boneless top loin roast (medium-low heat)	2 to 3 pounds (single loin) 3 to 5 pounds (double loin, tied)	1 to 1½ hours 1½ to 2¼ hours	150°F 150°F	160°F medium 160°F medium
Chop (boneless top loin)	¾ to 1 inch 1¼ to 1½ inches	20 to 24 minutes 30 to 35 minutes	160°F medium 160°F medium	No standing time No standing time
Chop (loin or rib)	¼ to 1 inch 1¼ to 1½ inches	22 to 25 minutes 35 to 40 minutes	160°F medium 160°F medium	No standing time No standing time
Country-style ribs		1½ to 2 hours	Tender	No standing time
Loin back ribs or spareribs		1½ to 1¾ hours	Tender	No standing time
Tenderloin (medium-high heat)	¾ to 1 pound	30 to 35 minutes	155°F	160°F medium

* All cooking times are based on meat removed directly from refrigerator.

DIRECT GRILLING BEEF*

CUT	THICKNESS/ WEIGHT	GRILLING TEMPERATURE	APPROXIMATE TIME	DONENESS
BEEF				
Boneless steak (beef top loin [strip], ribeye, shoulder top blade [flat-iron], tenderloin)	1 inch 1½ inches	Medium Medium	10 to 12 minutes 12 to 15 minutes 15 to 19 minutes 18 to 23 minutes	145°F medium rare 160°F medium 145°F medium rare 160°F medium
Boneless top sirloin steak	1 inch 1½ inches	Medium Medium	14 to 18 minutes 18 to 22 minutes 20 to 24 minutes 24 to 28 minutes	145°F medium rare 160°F medium 145°F medium rare 160°Fmedium
Boneless tri-tip steak (bottom sirloin)	¾ inch 1 inch	Medium Medium	9 to 11 minutes 11 to 13 minutes 13 to 15 minutes 15 to 17 minutes	145°F medium rare 160°F medium 145°F medium rare 160°F medium
Flank steak	1¼ to 1¾ pounds	Medium	17 to 21 minutes	160°F medium
Steak with bone (porterhouse, rib, T-bone)	1 inch 1½ inches	Medium Medium	10 to 13 minutes 12 to 15 minutes 18 to 21 minutes 22 to 25 minutes	145°F medium rare 160°F medium 145°F medium rare 160°F medium
GROUND MEAT				
Patties (beef, lamb, or veal)	½ inch ¾ inch	Medium Medium	10 to 13 minutes 14 to 18 minutes	160°F medium 160°F medium
KABOBS				
Beef, lamb, or veal	1-inch cubes 1½-inch cubes	Medium Medium	8 to 12 minutes 12 to 14 minutes	160°F medium 160°F medium

INDIRECT GRILLING BEEF*

CUT	THICKNESS/ WEIGHT	APPROXIMATE TIME	FINAL GRILLING TEMPERATURE (when to remove from grill)	FINAL DONENESS (after 15 minutes standing)
BEEF				
Boneless top sirloin steak	1 inch 1½ inches	22 to 26 minutes 26 to 30 minutes 32 to 36 minutes 36 to 40 minutes	145°F medium rare 160°F medium 145°F medium rare 160°F medium	No standing time No standing time No standing time No standing time
Flank steak	1¼ to 1¾ pounds	23 to 28 minutes	160°F medium	No standing time
Rib roast (chine bone removed) (medium-low heat)	4 to 6 pounds	2 to 2¾ hours 2½ to 3¼ hours	135°F 150°F	145°F medium rare 160°F medium
Steak (porterhouse, rib, ribeye, shoulder blade [flat-iron], T-bone, tenderloin, top loin [strip])	1 inch 1½ inches	16 to 20 minutes 20 to 24 minutes 22 to 25 minutes 25 to 28 minutes	145°F medium rare 160°F medium 145°F medium rare 160°F medium	No standing time No standing time No standing time No standing time
GROUND MEAT				
Patties (beef, lamb, or veal)	½ inch ¾ inch	15 to 18 minutes 20 to 24 minutes	160°F medium 160°F medium	No standing time No standing time

* All cooking times are based on meat removed directly from refrigerator.

DIRECT GRILLING POULTRY*

CUT	THICKNESS/WEIGHT	GRILLING TEMPERATURE	APPROXIMATE TIME	DONENESS
CHICKEN				
Chicken breast half, skinned and boned	4 to 5 ounces	Medium	12 to 15 minutes	170°F
Chicken thigh, skinned and boned	4 to 5 ounces	Medium	12 to 15 minutes	180°F
Meaty chicken pieces (breast halves, thighs, and drumsticks)	2½ to 3 pounds total	Medium	35 to 45 minutes	180°F
TURKEY				
Turkey tenderloin	8 to 10 ounces (¾ to 1 inch thick)	Medium	16 to 20 minutes	170°F

INDIRECT GRILLING POULTRY*

TYPE OF BIRD	WEIGHT	GRILLING TEMPERATURE	APPROXIMATE INDIRECT-GRILLING TIME	DONENESS
CHICKEN				
Chicken, whole	2½ to 3 pounds 3½ to 4 pounds 4½ to 5 pounds	Medium Medium Medium	1 to 1¼ hours 1¼ to 1¾ hours 1¾ to 2 hours	180°F 180°F 180°F
Chicken breast half, skinned and boned	4 to 5 ounces	Medium	15 to 18 minutes	170°F
Chicken thigh, skinned and boned	4 to 5 ounces	Medium	15 to 18 minutes	180°F
Meaty chicken pieces (breast halves, thighs, and drumsticks)	2½ to 3 pounds total	Medium	50 to 60 minutes	180°F
TURKEY				
Turkey, whole	6 to 8 pounds 8 to 12 pounds 12 to 16 pounds	Medium Medium Medium	1¾ to 2¼ hours 2½ to 3½ hours 3 to 4 hours	180°F 180°F 180°F
Turkey breast, half	2 to 2½ pounds	Medium	1¼ to 2 hours	170°F
Turkey breast, whole	4 to 6 pounds 6 to 8 pounds	Medium Medium	1¾ to 2¼ hours 2½ to 3½ hours	170°F 170°F
Turkey tenderloin	8 to 10 ounces (¾ to 1 inch thick)	Medium	25 to 30 minutes	170°F

* All cooking times are based on poultry removed directly from refrigerator.

Acknowledgments

It took the help of so many people to make this dream of mine possible. If I forgot anyone, please forgive me. I'll owe you a beer and a great home-cooked meal!

Dot DeStefano
Larry Anderson
David Antellocy
Aunt Sue
Chris Barron
Cindy Beaubien
Ron Brown
Kim Burke
Sharon Chobat
Coors Brewing
The Guys at Copperpost Production
Dick Dimming
Ken Easley and Randy Murray of First Studio
Kim Edoff
Dan Emery at Pilgrim's Pride Corporation (thanks for more than 10 years of the best chicken around)
Goodyear C.T.E. and C.T.W.
Goodyear Tire and Rubber Company
Robby Gordon
Tim Guiseppe
Rick Heinrich
Phil Holmer
James Hylton

Peter "Rabbit" Jellen
Chrissy Kernes
Kenney and Joan King
Tom & Beverly Koski
Kevin Lepage
Cindy Lewis
Meredith Manning
Sterling and Paula Marlin
Merrill Meyers
MERZ Project Architecture
John Millican
Susan Miller
Mike and Joe Motil
Kyle Petty
Richard Petty
Pilgrim's Pride Corporation
Rob Gerstner of Reel Men
David Riccobini
Felix and Carolyn Sabates
Jose Sabates
John Sands of Roush Racing
Jim Schoenberger
Lisa Scottford
Terry Shilkaitis
Bonnie Solow of Solow Literary
Tony Stewart
Bill Tybur
Jill Valdisar
John Venuti
Walt Smith of Whole Brain Films
John Woody

And a special thanks to Richard Bostic

Index